The Ultimate Guide for Exiting Your Business

TENSIE HOMAN & DAN MEYER

Copyright © 2013 by Execute on Strategy LLC.

All rights reserved. No part of this book may be used or reproduced in any manner whatsoever without written permission except in the case of brief quotations embodied in critical articles and reviews.

Published in the United States by Execute on Strategy LLC.

Cover design Copyright © 2013 – The Carlon Group

Graphics Copyright © 2013 – Renee Walker, Diverseye Design Inc.

Back cover photo by Edward DeCroce

Exit Bubble™ is a trademarked term of Execute on Strategy LLC.

ISBN: 978-0-615-77577-7

Library of Congress Control Number: 2013948598

Visit our website at: **www.ExitBubble.com**

Disclaimer

This publication is designed to provide information about the subject matter covered. The purpose of this book is to educate. It is not meant to take the place of experienced advisors in your exit process. We recommend you seek advice from qualified advisors throughout your exit process. Neither the authors nor Execute on Strategy LLC and affiliates shall have any liability or responsibility to any person or entity with respect to any loss or damage caused, or alleged to be caused, directly or indirectly by the information contained in this book.

This book comes with a FREE membership to ExitBubble.com

With this book, you receive *free of charge* access to valuable online resources and tools that would cost tens of thousands of dollars for you to obtain or create.

- Online valuation analysis tool that allows you to create multiple scenarios to value your business
- Video interviews of business owners and advisors on lessons learned and best practices related to the exit process
- Select webinars on timely and relevant topics for business owners
- Useful exit planning documents for all stages of your exit process

**To access your membership, go to
http://exitbubble.com/resources/booklevelmembership today.**

Acknowledgements

We'd like to thank everyone who has been with us through this journey with a special thanks to the following individuals who played important roles in making this book and ExitBubble.com possible.

Kelli Horst, who courageously agreed to edit a book written by two non-writers and did a brilliant job of making us sound like writers. The Carlon Group, who brought our book cover to life. Renee Walker of Diverseye Design Inc., who gave life to the pages of our book. Dirk and Matt at SteeleBoy Productions for making our videos look amazing.

Dustin Herman, who developed our valuation analysis tool. Selwa Hussain, who patiently guided us through the tax aspects of the book. Michele Gebhart, who took a leap of faith and joined our adventure. Bob Carrothers, who provided priceless coaching and advice.

To those who bravely read advance copies of this book and provided great feedback and insight: Stan Anders, Alex Cioth, David Cohn, Brian Cox, Tim Dumler, Jeff Feldman, Mira Fine, Scott Gesell, Lloyd Gottman, Mark Haden, Brad Hams, Ed Kelley, John Kelly, Carolyn Madero, Peter McLaughlin, Ralph Meyer, Don Spitzer and Mike Z.

And last, but not least, thank you to our families - Mike, Sara, Becca and Matt - for your love and trust.

What is the Exit Bubble™?

Five million baby boomers will be exiting their businesses over the next five years[1]. Ten million could exit over the next fifteen years[1]. We have the makings of a bubble, an Exit Bubble™. If you are a business owner, beware and be prepared!

During the recent housing bubble, competition for homebuyers was brutal for sellers. Only the best homes sold at a premium; fixer-uppers sold at losses, and those in the middle sat unwanted or were re-priced downward and sold below value. Like the housing bubble, the Exit Bubble™ will create a fiercely competitive environment for business owners competing to sell to a limited number of buyers.

What makes this even more frightening is that currently it is estimated only one in four owners successfully transfer their business to another owner, a trend that will likely get even worse during the Exit Bubble™.

This has real implications for your financial future. Nearly all baby boomer business owners plan to live on proceeds from the sale of their businesses when they retire, but 75% of those owners don't have a plan for exiting their

---

[1] See References

business[2]. Like most business owners, you've probably got up to 85% of your personal wealth tied up in your business, which leaves very little left over for savings. In fact, 65% of boomers have saved less than $100,000 for their retirement (and 40% have saved less than $10,000)[3].

Even if retiring isn't on your horizon just yet, you need to be thinking now about some of the critical issues you'll face in the future related to exiting your business if you hope to achieve your long-term financial and personal goals. You don't want to have to earn it again. In order to secure the future you have planned for you and your family, you need to beat the Exit Bubble™. We are going to show you how.

How to beat the Exit Bubble™

While you may never run a marathon, you can imagine that without preparation, training and knowing the course, running those 26.2 miles will cause you a lot of pain and injury, or worse. If you exit your business without properly preparing or understanding the roadmap, you'll risk experiencing the pain of lost control, financial injury, or failure to cross the finish line.

This book is your personal action plan to addressing the fundamental questions you need to ask yourself along the way to exiting:

- When should I exit my business?
- What are my exit strategies?
- What's my business worth?
- How do I exit my business?
- What will I do next?

2 See References
3 See References

In more than 25 years of accounting and transaction consulting, we have worked with companies of various sizes, industries and stages of maturity, as well as business owners with varying degrees of sophistication and experience. Repeatedly, we've seen sellers make critical mistakes that cost them significantly, slowed the process, or even killed their deal.

These mistakes were made primarily because business owners didn't prepare themselves and their businesses effectively or understand how to navigate the business exit process. We know these mistakes are avoidable.

As with most things in life, preparation and communication are the necessary ingredients to success. You must think through your goals and needs prior to engaging in an exit strategy. You need to learn to view your business and its value through the *eyes of the buyer* while controlling your emotions during this very lengthy and personal process. These are impossible challenges without the right preparation.

You want to gain every competitive advantage possible as a seller in the Exit Bubble™. You will need transaction advisors to keep you on even footing with potential buyers who are likely seasoned professionals at acquiring companies just like yours.

Do we want to be your transaction advisors or consultants? No! We have aggregated best practices from our own experiences and the experiences of hundreds of business owners, sellers, trusted advisors and buyers. By giving you an unbiased view on everything you'll face in this process, we are equipping you to navigate your journey with more control and achieve a more successful exit.

A lot of personal introspection and investment in your business needs to happen before you are ready to test the exit waters. You don't want to inadvertently cause the deal to die at the eleventh hour because you weren't prepared.

To beat the Exit Bubble™, you need a strategic understanding of the many steps involved in preparing yourself and your business to compete for the right buyer's attention and interest.

Who should read this book?

Whether you own a manufacturing company, a dentist office, a limousine service, an automotive repair shop, a bakery, a construction company, an accounting firm or any other type or size of business, you will need a plan to exit your business successfully. This book provides valuable and objective insights into the process of exiting your business.

Every business is different and every business owner is unique, but you can learn from the common themes and numerous lessons learned the hard way by owners of all business sizes and types as they have attempted to exit their businesses successfully.

Even if you consider yourself too small to need transaction advisors (investment bankers, brokers or attorneys) or plan to sell your business through an online business broker, you need to plan appropriately for what lies ahead.

This book will help you do many of the right things when you are ready to exit to make your business more valuable to the next owner, even if the idea of exiting your business is a distant thought.

How to read this book

Beat the Exit Bubble is the first comprehensive, go-to source detailing the entire lifecycle of exiting your business.

The book is separated into three parts that can be read in any order (but all parts are equally important to thorough preparation):

Part I - Prepare Yourself: identifying and evaluating your personal and financial goals, and how you might achieve them through various exit strategies

Part II - Prepare Your Business: estimating and maximizing the value of your business while learning to view your business through the eyes of the buyer

Part III - Exit Your Business: a step-by-step discussion of how the transaction is structured from start to finish, using "selling" as the exit strategy

Each part features ***Expert Insights*** and ***Gut Checks*** to call your attention to the most important takeaways from each step of the process. Even if you only skim the chapters for these helpful insights, you'll get a good sense of how much thought and preparation is necessary to navigate each stage of a successful exit.

Occasionally a word will appear in bold type and underlined, which means it is defined in the Glossary of Terms at the end of the book. The glossary is a collection of commonly used terms in the exit process. Take a few minutes to scan the glossary before you begin reading, or flip to the glossary when you come across a bold word to ensure you are comfortable with the meaning of the word.

Book Level Membership of **ExitBubble.com**

When you purchased this book, you became a Book Level Member of ExitBubble.com where you have access to an abundance of videos, tools and resources available on our website at www.ExitBubble.com *for no additional charge*. These resources include additional insights and lessons learned from business owners and advisors, access to webinars on important exit topics, and many other resources that are updated on a regular basis. You also have access to an online valuation tool that will allow you to run valuation scenarios using your business's information. You can conveniently access these resources online at **www.ExitBubble.com/booklevelmembership**.

Take it to the next level with Exit Bubble Elite

Your Book Level Membership, including *Beat the Exit Bubble*, introduces the wide range of issues and questions to consider as you familiarize yourself with the exit process, but it only scratches the surface of the detailed preparation and complex process you must undertake. Our online companion, Exit Bubble Elite, gives you additional, in-depth and hands-on tools to start answering those questions at your own pace before incurring significant transaction costs.

Exit Bubble Elite offers video case studies, personal coaching and interactive tools, including unlimited access to a customizable online valuation analysis tool. As a member of Exit Bubble Elite, you'll have the confidence to navigate the exit process successfully and become the one-in-four seller who beats the Exit Bubble™. Go to **www.ExitBubble.com** to learn more about Exit Bubble Elite.

Let's get started!

Table of Contents

What is the Exit Bubble™? v

Part I: Prepare Yourself 1

1 – Why do you need to prepare yourself? 2
2 – Prepare yourself emotionally 5
3 – Prepare yourself financially 8
4 – Prepare yourself NOW 17
5 – What are my exit options? 20
6 – Moving from "preparing yourself" to preparing your business 35

Part II: Prepare Your Business 39

7 – What does it mean to "prepare my business"? 40
8 – Who are my potential buyers? 42
9 – How do I estimate the value of my business? 49
10 – What's my business worth? 60
11 – What is my "Value Profile"? 77
12 – When do I pull the trigger on my exit? 84
13 – How do I improve my Value Profile? 89
14 – How do I implement and track my plan? 96
15 – Do I really need advisors? (Yes!) 100
16 – How do I control communication? 109
17 – Am I ready to move into the exit process? 122

Part III: Exit Your Business 125

18 – Entering the exit process 126
19 – Structuring your transaction 131

20 – Finding a buyer 147
21 – Phase I Diligence – the dance begins 156
22 – Negotiating the letter of intent 168
23 – Phase II Diligence – buckle your seatbelt! 181
24 – Closing – you beat the Exit Bubble™! 201

Exit Bubble Elite. 206

Glossary of Terms 209

References. 216

PART I

Prepare Yourself

"You plan everything in life, and then the roof caves in on you because you haven't done enough thinking about who you are and what you should do with the rest of your life."

– Lee Iacocca

1
Why do you need to prepare yourself?

Most seasoned transaction advisors agree that one of the top reasons, if not the number one reason, that business owners fail to sell their companies is: They aren't emotionally or financially prepared to <u>exit</u> their business. Talk to investment bankers or business brokers, and you'll hear plenty of stories about business owners backing out or blowing up the deal at the 11th hour.

Notice we use the word "exit" versus "sell." While related, there is a very important distinction between the two. *Exit* refers to any transition for the business owner out of or away from the business. This often means a *sale* of the business to a third party, but it can include other exit strategies discussed throughout this book.

Why is the notion of a transition so important? Most business owners build their company over decades, if not their entire working lives. They define themselves in terms of their business: "I'm the owner of the XYZ Company" or "I'm the president of ABC Corporation." Some may put it more modestly, with something like: "We own a little company that makes…" However they define themselves, many have a difficult time transitioning to who they are going to be and what they are going to do once they exit their company. Regardless of how you exit, sale or otherwise, you are in for some big changes.

While we all hope that change is for the better, these changes may not be so easy on you, your family or your business. Without preparation, you may find yourself adrift in unchartered life waters. You may need to access new skills or stretch yourself in other ways. As Peanuts creator Charles Schulz said, "Life is like a ten speed bicycle. Most of us have gears we never use." You need to make sure your "life gears" are properly tuned before entering this transition. This is the crux of preparing yourself for exit.

Be the one-in-four seller

In the introduction to this book, we referenced some scary statistics for business owners, including the prediction that only 25% of businesses up for sale will actually sell.

So, what does it take to be the one of those "one in four" who sells your business successfully? It all starts with you, the seller, preparing yourself effectively for this process and your life ahead.

In the *Seven Habits of Highly Effective People*, Steven Covey writes, "Begin with the end in mind." Make this your mantra. For most people, this is a very emotional process. You need to think about your desired emotional, as well as financial, outcomes. Underestimating the importance of preparation is an unnecessary risk, one that can cost you your life's work. You don't want to have to earn it again.

Ask yourself the right (and hard) questions

We know the first question you are going to ask: *What's my company worth?* We don't answer this question in *Part I* because, in our experience, that's not the first question you should be asking. You should be asking yourself these questions instead:

- Why am I really considering exiting my business?
- What are my exit goals - personal and financial?
- What exit strategy should I choose?
- When I am no longer a business owner, who am I?
- What will I do after the sale?
- How will this affect my family?

You need to prepare yourself by creating a clear vision of who you <u>are</u> and plan for who you will <u>be</u> next. If your response is to "play golf" or "travel," you could be setting yourself up for failure. You may have dreamt of playing golf in retirement, but what we are talking about is much deeper. Playing golf is something you <u>do</u>; it is not who you <u>are</u> or want to <u>be</u>.

> **Expert Insight:**
>
> ### Identity vs. Purpose
>
> Distinguishing your identity from your purpose is a critical consideration at this stage. You may have always identified yourself as "the owner of XYZ Company," so how will you react to the initial shock and withdrawal of no longer being that person? First, realize that person still exists! You are the same person with the same passion and drive as you were when you owned a company. You now have the opportunity to channel your energy into a purpose purely designed for personal happiness and fulfillment.

2
Prepare yourself emotionally

Who are you ... really?

Currently, you may see yourself as a CEO or an owner; or maybe you refer to yourself as a commercial printer, plastics manufacturer, chef, tire distributor, or dentist. Who will you be when you are no longer in that role? Sellers who haven't made an effort to answer this question honestly and thoughtfully will find the exit process even more daunting than it should be. They might also find their deals blowing up at the 11th hour.

Introspection is absolutely required if you want to be successful in your post-exit life. Begin to ask yourself questions such as:

- What are the values that are most important to me?
- How do I want to be remembered?
- What motivates me on a personal level?

As you start to think about <u>who</u> you are, you might find yourself thinking about <u>what</u> you do. You might be thinking that you're good at many things, but are you tapping into your natural strengths?

In order to succeed as a business owner, you have had to discipline yourself to be a better communicator, understand cash flow and balance sheets, negotiate contracts, be an effective sales manager, and even fill the role of HR manager. Do these activities really energize you, or are they what you had to do to survive and grow your business?

What activities do you perform in your work life today that you identify as your natural strengths? Have this conversation with your family and friends to get their input. Maybe engage in some formal assessments. Based on our personal experience, this may feel like a painful process; but when you discover the answers, it will be an eye-opening experience.

 **Gut Check: What gives you energy and a sense of purpose?**
Ask yourself questions such as:
- What am I naturally good at?
- What do I enjoy that feels effortless when I'm doing it?
- What do I truly love to do or dream of doing?
- What activities boost versus drain my energy?

The last question could be the key to unlocking who you want to be after you exit.

 **Online Resources: Understanding your natural strengths**

Retirement redefined - what other owners have experienced

We know former business owners who have gone on to teach fly fishing and golf (notice teach versus just play), gone back to school to become a chef, volunteered at the local homeless shelter, worked at their church in the mornings, and cared for their grandkids three days a week. You, alone, limit your choices and opportunities.

Sherri, a business owner, shared with us that her daughter was the one who pointed out to her that she was great at communicating with and developing her employees. She said, "Mom you'd be great at teaching." Sherri ended up selling her business and began teaching a couple of classes a year at her local college. Teaching the next generation of entrepreneurs and business leaders for her community energizes her, and she still has plenty of time to pursue her other passions.

Another business owner, Jerry, realized that while building his business he enjoyed analyzing and creatively solving complex problems he identified in his marketplace. He recalled when his kids were younger how much he enjoyed coaching his kids' soccer teams. Conversely, Jerry shared that as a result of preparing himself emotionally, he realized how much of an energy drain he experienced when working on accounting and HR issues. As part of his exit plan, Jerry now coaches small and middle-market business owners on strategic and operational issues. He's doing what gives him energy, and he has redefined himself post-exit.

This new lifestyle is referred to as *retirement redefined*. Research in this area shows that many people who retire to "nothing" experience dramatic decreases in quality of life, health and mental acuity. Don't leave yourself open to that risk.

 **Online Resources: Life Path worksheet**

3
Prepare yourself financially

Identifying the financial gap: where you are versus where you want to be

We know the majority of business owners are counting on the sale of their business to fund retirement – a key reason to make sure you are the one in four who sells your business successfully in the Exit Bubble™. We also know most business owners want to jump right to the part of the process that determines what their business is worth. Eventually, they came back to considering their financial plan.

Many owners will sell their business for a significant sum and have more than enough to fund their post-exit lifestyle. Why should they go through the financial planning process? For several reasons:

- It's important to develop a vision and expectation of what's ahead. Your family has lived with you through the ups and downs of your business all these years; it's worth including them in the planning process. They may have some important expectations of their own.
- Another reason a business owner with plenty of wealth should go through a formal financial planning process is to understand the principles of asset allocation, the benefit of different asset strategies, and the impact of income and estate taxes. Combine a big purchase, say a

second home, with a significant drop in the stock market, an increase in taxes, and inflation, and you may not be happy with your outcome. Remember, you don't want to have to earn it again!

Other business owners will have the opposite scenario on their hands. They may find that when adding the expected proceeds from the sale of their business into their financial plan, there is a gap between the amount of income they will have versus the amount of post-exit income they *want* or *need*. Many business owners have reinvested their profits back into their own business, leaving their savings lower than planned. No doubt, low-yet-volatile returns in the investment markets, forecasted inflation, rising tax rates, the post-exit cost of health care, and long-term care coverage are factors in this gap as well.

Estimating your post-exit financial needs

Exiting your business requires both a financial and an emotional transition. The financial transition may be more challenging than you'd expect, with health care, long-term care, car payments, mortgage(s), day-to-day bills, possibly children's college expenses, plus all the things you and your spouse want to do once you've exited your business. These expenditures seem to add up surprisingly fast once you no longer have that offsetting income stream from your business and you have more free time to spend money. Of course, there's also that little issue of how much cash you're really going to get if and when you sell your business after paying off debts, advisor fees and taxes.

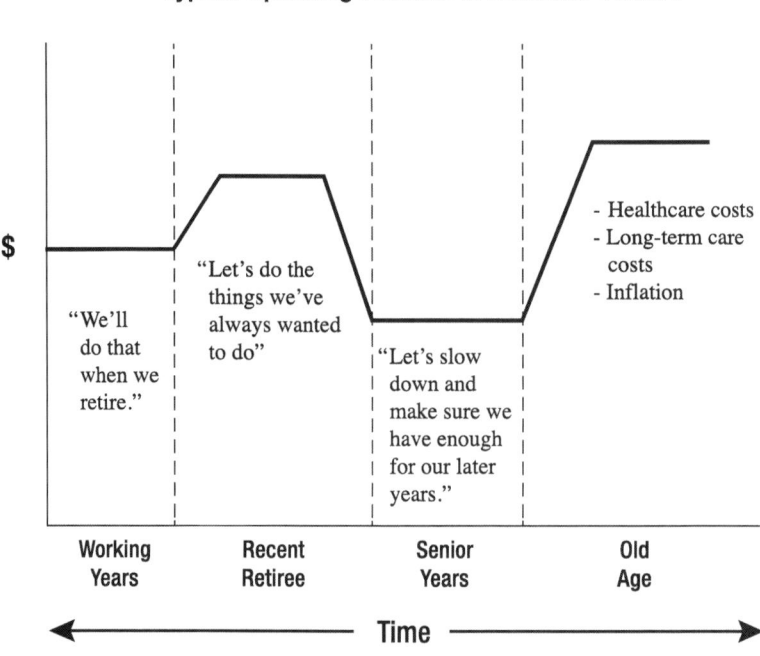

As you contemplate an exit of your business, you should consider the many financial benefits it has provided to you and your family over the years. Hopefully, during that time you've built valuable equity in your business that you can monetize in an exit. In addition to providing an income stream, your business may also cover the costs of health care for your family and education for your children. As your business became more successful, you may have bought cars for your spouse and kids, along with other tangible perks associated with owning your own business. This is a common practice for business owners, and these are real benefits that are likely to cease if you sell your business.

We address all of the personal assets and expenses that might flow through your financials in *Part II*. For now, let's focus on ensuring you are financially prepared to replace the income stream and these other benefits in your post-exit financial plan. It's possible that a sale of your business will generate more than enough cash for you to live the retirement life of your dreams. It's also very likely that, without proper planning, it won't. Let's start by estimating the cash impact to you when you exit your business.

Today, financial advisors have tools that can model your retirement financial needs through various scenarios. These tools enable you to understand the impact of varying investment amounts (cash from exit + other savings/investments), risk/return allocations, spending, taxes, inflation, and much more. The goal of working with an advisor and using these tools is not to determine your net worth based on assumptions of your business value. Rather, the goal is to understand what resources you will need post-exit to replace your income stream and benefits for the rest of your life. The goal is also to establish a plan for generating income based on the value of your business under different exit scenarios.

As an example, a rancher may own hundreds or even thousands of acres of land worth millions of dollars and therefore has an attractive net worth. The problem is that the rancher may not be able to cover day-to-day living expenses for retirement if the land isn't generating any cash flow. In order to generate cash flow for income, the rancher may have to lease the land to someone else or sell off parcels. Just like in running your business, cash flow is king in planning for your personal financial future!

Often, business owners will perform a great deal of financial planning on their own. That being said, when you are creating your financial plan for exit, it is vital you include your family and advisors in the process. We all have wants, needs and blind spots that need to be identified and considered.

If you *Google* the term "retirement calculator," you'll find an extensive list of free resources available on the Internet. You'll see that while some are more complex than others, each has pluses and minuses, so you might try several tools to get different perspectives. Of course, none of the calculators will give you the same result. Why? The results from any of these tools are just estimates; therefore, it's better to be more conservative than overly optimistic with your analysis.

If your conservative analysis provides you a satisfactory outcome, it is probable that under more attractive market conditions (higher or more consistent returns, lower outflows or costs) the results of your analysis will look even better.

 **Online Resources: Personal Vault checklist**

The role of financial advisors

In working with a financial advisor, there should be no doubt in your mind this person has the right skills and is willing to help you with your post-exit financial analysis. Advisors should be able to provide ideas and perspective as you develop your personal exit plan. To be most effective in this role, your financial advisor needs the full breadth and depth of experience to support you in your exact situation.

Charlie, the former owner of a manufacturing company, had a small IRA account and the company's small 401K with his financial advisor. This was actually his wife's IRA and accounted for their entire net worth outside of the equity in his business. When Charlie sold the business, his account grew to over $10 million. Unfortunately, his current financial advisor was way out of his league in managing that type of wealth. Charlie stayed with him because the advisor wisely partnered with another professional in his firm who worked with higher net worth clients.

It's important that you select your financial advisor based on how they can serve your future needs, not just your current or past needs. The same applies to other legal or accounting advisors you may engage. For example, it will be important to have a certified public accountant (**CPA**) or multiple CPAs with the appropriate transaction accounting and tax expertise on your team. While you might have a CPA who files your tax returns, an exit transaction is different and may require you to find a different CPA with specialized knowledge. We appreciate your respect and loyalty for your current CPA but, depending on the size of your transaction, making a change is worth considering. You can always go back to your CPA next year for tax filings or other services.

> **Expert Insight:**
> ### Who should be my financial advisor?
> Don't automatically assume that your current financial advisor, CPA or attorney is the right resource to assist you effectively in managing your finances in your post-exit life. Select your advisor based on how they can serve your current and future needs, not just on your past relationships.

We discuss transaction advisors more in *Part II*. For now, consider who you already have available to support you on planning and executing an exit. Before you engage them, make sure they have the appropriate experience to be a valuable part of your team.

Show me the money!

How do you estimate how much money you'll actually get if you exit? That amount will depend on the valuation of your business and the structuring of your transaction. Many business owners have in mind a rough idea of the sales price for their business. This price may be based on conversations with business brokers, other owners who have sold their companies, competitors who have exited over the past few years and received the infamous "five times **EBITDA** (earnings before interest, taxes depreciation and amortization)," among other valid and not-so-valid sources.

If you dig deeper, sellers who have successfully sold their business will tell you that it would have been pure coincidence if the sale price actually matched the target value they had originally established early in the process. Valuation, structuring and estimating the cash you may receive in an exit is another area where good transaction advisors can be very helpful.

While valuation and the estimated cash you may receive in an exit is important, it is only half of the equation. You will want to consider how your valuation compares to your post-exit financial needs.

What to do when you come up short

The biggest reason you may have a gap in desired and actual future income is that, after going through your business valuation calculation, you realize your business may not be worth as much as you had hoped. If this is the case, what are your options? If you still want to exit and you have a gap in desired and actual income, you have four options: 1) increase your income (this may mean increasing the value of your business prior to exit) 2) run the business for a few more years and incorporate an aggressive savings plan 3) reduce your personal costs or 4) a combination of all of the above.

>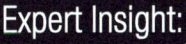
> **Expert Insight:**
> **Downshifting as a strategy**
> The strategy of reducing your personal costs (and possibly your lifestyle) post-exit is a lot more common than you might think. In the mid-2000s, a significant portion of retirees hadn't put enough away for retirement and counted on the equity in their home to close the gap. That strategy was upended by the housing bubble, the stock market meltdown of 2008, and the uncertainty that followed.

If you find yourself needing to reduce your personal costs to close a financial gap, you're not alone. You should become familiar with a new term, **downshifting**. Some boomers are downshifting in order to save more money and have enough for their retirement years. A great many more are pursuing this lifestyle by choice. They're trading in their McMansions for smaller, well-designed homes that will better meet their needs in retirement. It's possible that, in a few more years, when boomers look to exit their larger homes en masse, there will be a glut of McMansions for sale. The next generation is smaller in population and, on average, can't afford them. That's something to consider in your transition plan.

Downshifters will typically continue to work, at least part-time, in the new age of retirement redefined. This might mean scaled-back work in their current business or it could mean working for someone else. The current trend shows some are consulting in their former area of expertise. Others reinvent themselves to pursue something more closely aligned with their life-long passions. Still others are working in a job that gets them out of the house and makes enough extra income to cover the costs of visiting the grandkids or pay for a vacation each year. It can be quite invigorating if the new "what you do" is well-synched with those things that give you energy and more closely define "who you are."

 **Gut Check: Would downshifting improve your quality of life?**

If downshifting is going to be part of your exit strategy, think about what steps you and your family could take toward making this new lifestyle an attractive reality. As you contemplate what downshifting might mean for you and your family, ask yourself these questions:

- What am I trying to achieve with downshifting: aligning day-to-day life with natural strengths, passions and interests; long-term financial security; better health, more free time?
- What is my plan for gradual downshifting: reduce day-to-day living expenses, right-size my home, focus on "quality of life" versus "keeping up with the Jones's?"
- What is my emergency downshifting plan if I or someone in my family becomes ill?
- Is my family aligned with this choice of lifestyle?

4
Prepare yourself NOW

Can't I sort out my emotions and financials later?

Not if you want to beat the Exit Bubble™! It is tempting to put off the emotional and financial self-preparation we recommend. After all, as a business owner, you are very busy and you'd rather deal with it after the deal is done, right?

Preparing yourself is about more than positioning for a post-exit life. It is a critical element in being able to execute an exit, especially a sale to a third party.

Even if you feel you are 100% emotionally and financially prepared for exit, if you can't convincingly communicate that to potential buyers, they may walk away before you've finished your first meeting. Potential buyers will not want to waste any time on acquiring a business from an owner they believe might blow up the deal late in the process. Remember, you may be competing with other sellers for limited buyers in the Exit Bubble™. Having a well thought-out exit plan will appeal to potential buyers and increase their confidence in pursuing a deal with you.

Why are you exiting?

Understanding and accepting your own answer to this question are fundamental to achieving your successful exit. Equally important is your communication about the transition. Once you have clarity, you'll be able to develop a clear and appropriate message to share consistently with others when the time is right.

> **Expert Insight:**
>
> ### Don't let a buyer catch you off guard
>
> Experienced buyers will repeatedly weave the "exit topic" into their meetings and conversations with a business owner. Expect a prospective buyer to ask these primary questions early in the process: "Why are you selling your business?" Or, "What do you think you'll do after you exit?" You should also expect to be asked about your financial preparedness and plans for after the sale. Do they really care? Yes. They want to make sure that if they invest the time, attention and money pursuing the purchase of your business, you are equally committed to getting the transaction completed.

Your reasons for exiting, and how you communicate that reason, should be considered early in the process. You might ask yourself the following questions:

- Do I *want* to exit, or do I *have* to exit?
- What's driving my decision to exit?
    - ❒ My age and retirement
    - ❒ Health reasons: self or family member
    - ❒ Financial reasons
    - ❒ I've taken the company as far as I can

- ❏ My family tells me it's time to retire
- ❏ I'm burned out
- ❏ I've made enough money and am ready for something else

> **Expert Insight:**
>
> ### Why are you exiting?
>
> Regardless of your actual reason for exiting, you need to communicate your message consistently and predictably during the exit process. We address communication in detail later in Part II. How you frame your message needs to be thoughtful and professional. Keep it real, but think about how you will say it and then practice it out loud in your car or with a family member or friend to get it down.

5
What are my exit options?

Everybody exits eventually

The five primary exit strategies fall into two categories, proactive and passive. Regardless of who you are or what type of business you own, all business owners exit their business in one of the following ways:

Proactive exit strategies:
1. Sell to a third party
2. Sell to existing employees
3. Transition to next generation

Passive exit strategies:
4. Fade away
5. Feet first and horizontal (work to your last breath)

The "proactive" exit strategies

Options 1, 2 and 3 require more proactive planning and decision-making on your part.

As we've pointed out, currently only one in four businesses sell successfully. There are many factors contributing to this low success rate, among them sellers who are unprepared for the emotional and physical stress of preparing their business for sale and going through the sale process itself. The process can be compared to the ups and downs of a roller coaster ride, but this time it's an emotional roller coaster.

Our intention is not to scare you off or dissuade you from selling. To the contrary, our objective is to give you the vision and tools necessary to navigate the exit process by identifying the risks and creating an action plan on how to address those risks. We want to help your emotional roller coaster go from the "Mind Eraser" to the "Kiddie Koaster," no matter the type of buyer.

In selling to your employees or transitioning to the next generation, it's advisable to treat your employees or next generation as a third-party buyer to ensure fair valuation and supportable documentation for tax and legal purposes. *Part III* of this book, which focuses primarily on selling your business, can be used as a guide for all proactive exit strategies.

Option 1 - sell to a third party

The most common exit strategy for business owners looking to fund their retirement needs is to sell to a third party. Although this option provides the best opportunity to generate cash at exit, it can also be the most emotionally difficult exit process for a business owner. Selling your life's work to a stranger can be challenging especially if you're not prepared for the **diligence** process and the deal negotiations. Having a clear view of what you'll do after you sell your business to a third party will help you maintain a sense of control during the sale process. We discuss the process of selling to a third party in *Part III*.

Expert Insight:

Going public

Some business owners might consider taking their company public through an initial public offering ("IPO"). This option might seem exciting to some, but you should be aware of the some of the challenges of being a public company as well as how it impacts your ability to actually exit your business.

- The process of going public and the cost to comply with all the regulations of a public company are significant and will require additional infrastructure.
- You'll suddenly be answering to multiple shareholders who may not have the same vision for your company's future.
- You may not be able to exit the business once it becomes public as shareholders generally invest in the CEO who is expected to continue in the business.
- There will be restrictions on when you can actually sell your stock and receive proceeds which may impact your future plans.

Going public is more often considered a growth strategy versus an exit strategy. Make sure you understand all of the positives and negatives of becoming a publicly traded company before you choose that option.

> **Expert Insight:**
>
> ## You need a formal process to transition to family or employees
>
> While there will be some legal and accounting costs incurred, the benefits of going through a formal process of transitioning your business to your management team or next generation often outweigh the costs. Both parties want to feel like they got a fair deal no matter who they are. Depending on the size and complexity of the transaction, you may consider including a formal valuation in the transaction process to create clarity for both parties. A formalized transaction process also provides legal and estate planning benefits to you, the seller.

Options 2 and 3 – sell to employees or transition to next generation

Whether you're selling to existing employees or transitioning to the next generation, you may be facing similar issues as you would with an external buyer.

1. "Will I get enough cash to achieve my exit goals?"

If you expect to get a full or partial lump sum payment from your management team or family who are taking over the business, where will the money come from?

Typically, your employees or family will not have the funds on hand to buy the business. If receiving a lump sum is the strategy of choice, you'll need to create a way for your buyers to accumulate the cash to buy you out. There are many ways to fund this option, including deferred compensation or cash value life insurance.

These programs require you, the owner, to establish a process for funding many years in advance. It can take anywhere from five to ten or even 15 years for your family or employees to accumulate the funds necessary for a buyout. If you're not planning to exit your business in the near term, you can learn more about these cash value accumulation strategies by talking with your CPA, financial advisor or life insurance representative.

Although these financial strategies are fairly common, it is critical that you work with a trusted advisor who understands the nuances and can articulate them to you clearly. How the program is structured will determine who owns the assets: the company or the employee. If the assets belong to the company, they may be lost if the company is sued or goes bankrupt. If the assets belong to the employee or family member, there is no guarantee they will use the money to buy your business when you want to exit. They could use the money to buy a new home, invest it somewhere else, or go work at another company.

2. "How will my employees or next generation finance the purchase?"

Can your employees or family borrow the money to purchase the business?

If this is the strategy of choice, the lender will consider the cash flow of the business, the credit quality of the borrowers, and the down payment contributed by the buyers. When using this strategy, it is important to understand who is in the first position for the assets if the acquiring employees can't meet their obligations. It is also essential to consider the impact of changing interest rates and tax rates on the business' cash flows to determine if the numbers work in the long term.

Will your employees or family buy you out over time? If so, what percentage of the deal are you willing to finance?

This is another way of saying that you are the "bank" and will receive a stream of payments over time. The primary benefits of this exit strategy are you know your buyer(s) and you may pay fewer income taxes on the transaction (i.e., future annual payments may keep you in a lower tax bracket than if you had received a bigger lump sum payment today).

This may also be the only form of retirement income you have available. The downside is that, as the lender, you carry the risk of the buyer (borrower) defaulting. There are many stories of both successes and failures related to this strategy.

There is much more to learn about this topic, and you may be asking yourself, "Why, if I'm simply transitioning to family or selling to employees, would I go through the effort of preparing my business as you recommend?"

> ### Gut Check: Treating employees or family like any other buyer
>
> You trust them; you love them ... so why should you treat them like any other buyer? Consider these questions:
> - Is your intent to maximize the exit value of your business and therefore your payment stream?
> - Is the certainty of that payment stream critical to your financial security in your retirement?
> - Are the long-term image of your business, the respect of your employees, and appreciation of your customers and suppliers important factors in your legacy?
>
> If you answered "yes" to any of these questions, you need to take emotion out of the equation and ensure a fair outcome for all parties by treating your employees and/or family members with the same professionalism as you would external buyers.

The transition from employee to owner is significant and can be challenging. If you prepare your business properly, you will have improved the capability and performance of the individuals taking over the leadership roles of the company. You will also have improved the financial and operational excellence of your business. Ultimately, your organization will more likely continue to thrive after your departure.

Is an ESOP a viable tool for financing?

Another option for transitioning your business to your employees or management team is to create an **Employee Stock Ownership Plan** (**ESOP**). ESOPs create a "private" market for company stock and are sponsored by the company. The company makes pretax contributions to the ESOP, and then uses the funds in the ESOP to purchase the owner's stock upon exit. Because the payments to the selling owner are pretax, it takes a smaller amount of funds than a direct sale to management.

One of the potential benefits of using an ESOP is to ensure the continuation of the company after the owner has transitioned the company to family or employees. Cash flow is critical in planning for exit in an ESOP, as the company must fund the owner's exit payments while maintaining enough cash to support the company's growth plans.

> **Expert Insight:**
>
> **ESOPs require a strong balance sheet**
> One of the challenges with ESOPs is that the business might need to borrow the money to buy the owner's stock, thereby leveraging the business. If the business doesn't have a strong balance sheet, that leverage could limit growth of the business in the future. Make sure you understand how the ESOP will be funded when planning for this option.

An ESOP is governed by the IRS and Department of Labor and can be complex to set up and maintain. We highly recommend getting a qualified advisor involved in the process if you decide on this option.

3. "What will my post-exit involvement be?"

How can you tell if your next generation or management team is ready to take over the business?

One business owner we worked with put it this way: "Let's say over the past one or two years, you have reduced your time at the business to two or three days a week and you take a two- to four-week vacation with minimal calls and e-mail. When you return, if the business is still running great, you have the basis for success. If not, you just don't know what the outcome will be."

We often see business owners transition the company to their employees or family only to have to return to the business a few years later because the new owners weren't prepared or capable of running the business. If you plan to transition your business to employees or family, make sure you have performed a rigorous assessment of their abilities to effectively run the business so you don't risk having to return, or worse, not getting the cash flows you expected when you originally exited.

> **Gut Check: Am I ready to transition to employees or my family?**
>
> Some questions you need to answer honestly:
> - How strong is the management team that is buying the business?
> - What is my financial dependency related to the business' continued success? If I pass away before the agreed term of the payments, does my spouse or estate continue to receive payments?
> - At what frequency, if any, will I have access to information related to the performance and financials of the business?
> - What course of action can or will I take if the business starts underperforming?
> - What does underperforming mean? Does it mean the same thing to me as it does to my buyer?
> - If the buyer(s) fails to meet the financial obligations, am I willing or capable of taking the company back and running it?
>
> Ask the hard questions now so you don't find yourself as a business owner planning your exit strategy a second time.

The "passive" exit strategies

Passive exit strategies (options 4 and 5) are those you let happen versus those you proactively execute.

Option 4 – fade away

"Fade away" simply means you've decided to gradually scale back your business versus transitioning it to another owner. Under this exit strategy, little by little, the business fades away until nothing remains. While this sounds like a terrible thing, it makes good sense for many business owners by fulfilling a *need*, a *want*, or *both*.

For example, consider a financial advisor who manages her retired clientele's investments. She has grown her business through word of mouth, and she is now considering retirement herself. While she could sell her book of business to another advisor, she has no intention of doing so. Her plan for exiting is to let her client base shrink over time while she continues working fewer and fewer hours for her clients who remain. She loves what she does, cares for her clients, and can't bear the thought of entrusting their investments to someone else. At the same time, she has no interest in trying to add new clients. She realizes that at some point, she may have no clients at all, and her income stream will cease. She has chosen the fade away option for exiting her business. In this case, her finances (savings) support this option, and it is what she *wants* to do.

Another example is a self-employed environmental consultant who wants to retire or at least slow down a bit to spend more time with the family. He doubts that he could sell his business because *he* is the business. He realizes that even if a sale was possible, it would not generate an income stream sufficient to support many years of retirement. He chooses to gradually scale back his client base and work a little less each year. This allows him to continue to generate some income but free up time for the family. He will continue to cut back in future years and, little by little, his business will fade away.

In both examples, the owners planned for their exit, ensuring their finances were sufficient to support them in retirement. Fade away does not mean let things go without a plan. You still must plan to ensure you meet your retirement needs.

Some business owners *need* some continuing income or benefits from their business while others simply *want* a continuing role with the business. Regardless of the reasons for pursuing this exit option, it is a common and viable strategy when you plan for it.

Option 5 – feet first and horizontal

Feet first and horizontal (the owner dies without a formal succession plan and the business goes on life support) can happen to any of us, at any time. The key takeaway is business owners must prepare for its possibility. Sadly, many avoid the mere thought of death.

As a business owner, it is likely many people depend on you every day. Your employees, customers, suppliers and even creditors need you around – or at least your business. You don't want to leave them in a lurch when you are gone. Think about how your business, in your absence, will pull itself off life support and continue to thrive for the people who need it. It won't do it on its own. It will need someone from your management team to take charge in your absence. Assignments must be known and communicated for an effective transition of power.

For the sake of your employees, customers, suppliers and general legacy, you need clear, well-communicated succession plans and, perhaps, incentives for key employees to stay ("golden handcuffs"). What will it take to keep your business running effectively after you are gone?

Don't forget about your family! As a business owner, your family probably depends on you. Your business is the income-generating machine for your loved ones. If you are gone, how will that business continue to provide income for your family?

Will it be sold off and the net proceeds paid to your family or estate? Will your family or estate be able to capture earnings from the business in some way? How can you arrange ahead of time for your family to continue to have an income stream in the event you are no longer here? This is an important conversation to have with your CPA, financial advisor and life insurance representative, as well as with your loved ones.

Then there's the matter of estate taxes. How will your loved ones deal with the tax consequences of your passing? While you might be out of the picture, you need to realize the IRS will want their estate tax money from the value of your business. Where will the money come from? The IRS doesn't care; it's your family's problem. Interestingly, even the wealthy miss this one. Adolf Coors passed away without proper planning for his business and estate. During the time that should have been reserved for grieving, the Coors family had to take the beer dynasty public in order to pay the taxes—probably not what the founder had dreamed would happen.

These are all important matters, and you should think seriously about estate planning for your family.

> **Gut Check: Have you planned for the worst case scenario?**
>
> You have invested yourself and your money into building your business. You have earned the respect and trust of family, employees, customers and suppliers. Don't lose all that from lack of preparation for a feet first and horizontal exit.
>
> Have you planned appropriately so you leave behind a great legacy, rather than great problems?

"Passive" doesn't mean you shouldn't plan

You would think that options 4 and 5 would be easy to deal with. They're "passive," so you shouldn't have to do anything, right? Wrong! While planning may not affect you, the business owner, it will dictate what happens to your family and business if something unexpected occurs. You can't predict what will happen to you or someone in your family that might change your ability or desire to continue running your business. Plan ahead to protect your family's income and your business' leadership.

We knew a successful business owner, Carl, who was satisfied with his situation and planned to work several more years. Unexpectedly, his wife became ill and he needed to move her to a different climate. Suddenly, it became more important to focus on her medical needs than his business. Carl had always been healthy and hadn't thought about the impact an illness in his family might have on his future plans and his business. No one on his management team was capable of becoming the CEO, and he couldn't find a suitable person to hire quickly. The outcome? Carl sold his company at a deep discount, significantly impacting his overall financial situation and making it difficult to pay for his wife's medical care. The business he had owned for 30 years was not prepared to survive without him as the CEO and, within a year, it closed its doors.

Estate planning and succession planning are critical for every business owner, whether you experience a passive or proactive exit. Like discussing life insurance, this type of planning isn't a pleasant exercise, but it's necessary to protect your family and business after you're gone—and worth the peace of mind. These are areas where advisors can be very helpful, if not critical, to deal with your own unique situations. Failure to address the issue head-on can be very costly to your family.

> **Gut Check: Estate planning**
> - Will your surviving family need the funds they inherit from you for their day-to-day living expenses?
> - How will you transfer your values and your wealth to the next generation?
> - What about your estate plan? If you don't think you have enough wealth to need one, remember that at death we are all charitable. With planning, you choose how you'll be charitable to your family and your community (church, synagogue, alma mater). Without proper planning, you'll still be charitable, but it may be to the government (in the form of taxes).
>
> Spend time answering these questions while you still have the ability to impact the outcome!

Succession planning – how will your business survive you?

As you begin to think through your succession plan, consider the following issues:

- Is there a natural successor already on the management team? Have you started training him or her to take over your role?
- If not already in the company, how will you identify and hire a successor?
- Depending on the size of your business, you may need to establish a leadership transition plan and a financial transition plan. Your legal and tax advisor can help you formulate this strategy. Once created, your leadership team should be made aware of your plans.

- Your leadership team can support you in communicating appropriately to your employees, customers, suppliers, creditors and other stakeholders.

After exploring your exit options, it's okay if you decide not to exit right now. If your decision, for now, is to keep your business, you'll still exit one way or another at some point in the future. ExitBubble.com can be a valuable resource to you, personally and financially, while you're still running your business.

6
Moving from "preparing yourself" to "preparing your business"

Increasing the sale value of your business = increasing post-exit income

Earlier, we stated the first way to close the post-exit financial gap is to increase income by increasing the sale price of your business. Maybe you are the business owner who doesn't have a financial gap, but you are committed to selling your business for the highest price possible—and you have the discipline and energy to prepare your business for sale. In this regard, selling a business is similar to selling a home. The sellers who take the time to improve and stage their home, making it more attractive to prospective buyers, usually have better outcomes than those who don't. You have the advantage when you take the time to "stage" your business.

What's different than selling a home is how long it takes to improve or "stage" a business. Not only do you have to put improvements in place, but you need time to show the impact of those improvements. That's why it's critical to start preparing your business as early as possible.

Working *on* your business versus working *in* it

One of the most common lessons learned by those who have successfully exited – and those who haven't – is the need for a mindset shift from working *in* the company to working *on* the company. This means a change in focus for owners from selling products to selling an entire business.

Once you make that mindset shift, you'll begin to ask yourself questions such as:

- What's my company worth?
- Who else do I need to involve in the sale process?
- How do I prepare my business to get the price I want or need?

Parts II and *III* will help you answer these questions.

> **Key takeaways from Part I – Prepare yourself:**
> - Prepare yourself financially *and* emotionally to exit your business
> - Understand *who* you are versus *what* you do
> - Select your financial advisor based on your future needs, not your current needs
> - Downshifting may be an important option for you
> - Consider your reasons for exiting and effectively communicate those early in the process
> - Understand all of your potential exit options. Starting early allows you to pursue multiple exit options enabling you to make your final decision when the timing is right.
> - Estate *and* succession planning are key to a successful exit under any option

Online resources referenced in Part I:

Buying this book gives you *free access* to online resources available through your Book Level Membership of **ExitBubble.com**, including, but not limited to, the resources referenced in *Part I*:

- Understanding your natural strengths
- Life Path worksheet
- Personal Vault checklist

Go deeper in Exit Bubble Elite

Exit Bubble Elite provides you in-depth and personalized resources such as:

- Emergenetics profile – customized exclusively for Exit Bubble Elite.
    - ❏ A personalized assessment of your natural strengths by Emergenetics International, a company specializing in analyzing, identifying and leveraging the way people think and behave.
    - ❏ Includes a one-on-one coaching session with a Certified Emergenetics Associate who can help you identify and understand your natural strengths and begin to answer "who am I, if I'm not the owner of my business?"
- Life Path Workbook - exclusive to Exit Bubble Elite
    - ❏ Hands-on exercises that will help you apply what you learned through your Emergenetics profile to your plans for "post-exit" life.
- Personal Vault
    - ❏ In-depth tool that warehouses all of your critical information in one place, including all of your passwords, financial information, insurance information, and other information you or family may need in a moment's notice.

PART II

Prepare Your Business

"Even if you are on the right track, you'll get run over if you just sit there."

– Will Rogers

7
What does it mean to "prepare my business"?

In *Part I*, you began the process of understanding what you need to consider for the next phase of life after business ownership. This included an evaluation of your financial situation and an assessment of your personal needs ("what gives you energy?" and "who will you be?").

While these are issues related to your life *after* ownership, addressing these matters *prior* to exiting is paramount to your success. Considering these issues *now* is important because not doing so often creates unnecessary problems that can complicate, delay, or even jeopardize an exit, especially if you intend to sell your business.

It is equally important to prepare your business *prior* to beginning your exit process. So what exactly does that mean?

If you were thinking of selling your house, you would try to estimate what it is worth and how much money you would receive after paying off the mortgage and paying realtor fees and closing costs. Obviously, the hope is that you can walk away with enough cash to put toward your next dream home or a vacation home.

Homeowners who understand how to catch the interest of buyers and get the highest possible sales price prepare their homes before putting them on the market by making repairs, painting and decluttering. Why would you approach exiting your business any differently, especially in the Exit Bubble™?

Preparing your business means taking a hard look at your business in ways you may never have before. It means you work *on* your business rather than *in* it. It means you begin the process of gathering financial information that potential buyers will need to assess the value of your business. It means you estimate the value of your business, deciding what you can and will do to increase its value prior to starting the exit process.

This can be hard work, especially while continuing to run your business. It's work that many business owners never do, or work they delay until they are deep into the exit process. By then, it is too late to leverage the real power and competitive advantage that preparation and communication would have given you at the deal table.

Part II, "Prepare Your Business," will help you answer the following questions as you contemplate your exit strategy and timing:

- Who are my potential buyers?
- How do I estimate the value of my business?
- How do I maximize the value of my business?
- When do I pull the trigger on my exit?
- How and when do I engage advisors?
- What is a communication plan?
- Am I ready to exit?

8
Who are my potential buyers?

At first, you may want to answer this question with, "I have no idea and I don't see why it matters!" or "Right now, I am more interested in figuring out what my business is worth." If this was your reaction, you are not alone; but ultimately, the value of your business depends on who is buying it and what they think your business is worth to them.

How many times have you heard "it's worth what someone is willing to pay for it?" That doesn't seem helpful if you are trying to determine what your business is worth *prior* to deciding to exit or knowing who your potential buyer is.

When you prepare a home for sale, the improvements and changes you make should focus on how a potential buyer might see them, not necessarily how you see them. The same holds true for preparing your business for exit. You must view your business through the *eyes of the buyer* and take steps to make your business as attractive as possible to the next owner. Although you won't know for sure who your buyer will be at this point in the process, understanding the traits and motivations of different types of buyers will help you identify value drivers and value detractors of your business throughout this process.

> **Expert Insight:**
>
> **Looking through the eyes of the buyer**
>
> In the 1st century, B.C., the Latin writer Publilius Syrus said, "Everything is worth what its purchaser will pay for it." Even then, the importance of viewing a product or business through the eyes of the buyer was recognized. For a business owner facing the Exit Bubble™, that means understanding how a potential buyer will value your business before you enter the sale process.

One type of buyer is not necessarily better than another, but each may value your company differently based on their strategy and motivations for your business after the sale. We classify buyers into three primary types: strategic, financial and lifestyle.

For example, say you own a retail business with three locations in your city. Your potential buyers might take the following views:

- A **strategic buyer** might be a competitor with one location in your town and four locations in a neighboring town. This buyer will value your business based on the incremental revenues from the additional locations, but may also plan on cost savings by consolidating the administrative functions of the two companies and eliminating a good portion of your team.
- A **financial buyer** might be looking at your business as a first acquisition in the industry with ideas of acquiring and consolidating your competitors into your business. This buyer will be very interested in the quality of your management team to continue running the business and whether you have an infrastructure that can support growth in the future (i.e., a platform for growth).

- A **lifestyle buyer** might look at it as a way to make a nice living for the remainder of his or her career. This buyer will be concerned with the quality of existing management to continue running the business smoothly and the predictability of cash flows to support the desired lifestyle. This buyer might also be interested in **seller financing**.

Let's discuss each type of buyer in a little more detail.

Strategic buyers

Strategic buyers generally already own a company in your industry or a complementary industry, and they are looking to expand their product line, geography, customer base, or overall market share. A challenge with understanding how strategic buyers will value your business is that each of them has their own unique reason for wanting to purchase your business.

Strategic buyers who believe that your product or service, geographic footprint or technology will significantly increase their market share and give them a competitive advantage most likely will not care as much about the historical or projected results of your business on a stand-alone basis. They're looking at what your product will do for their existing business going forward. For strategic buyers, it's the strategic fit that matters.

For example, one of our former clients, Mark, owned a technology business and performed several valuations on his company. He estimated, along with the help of advisors, the value to be around $40 million. A strategic buyer who needed to add Mark's product to its own product to be competitive paid more than $100 million for the business. There was no logical or mathematical way for Mark to estimate the $100+ million value because there was an intangible, future value to the buyer of which he was not aware.

> **Expert Insight:**
>
> ### Know your value to potential buyers
>
> Get to know your potential buyers and how they are valuing your business prior to accepting an offer. We've seen sellers who have not understood how valuable their product or technology was to a strategic buyer because they didn't talk to the buyer about plans for the business after the sale. They potentially left millions of dollars on the table. Don't let this happen to you. Get to know your buyer and understand how your business fits into their overall strategy.

When a strategic buyer is a current competitor of yours, special challenges arise. You'll need to be sensitive to disclosing competitive information too early in the process. Customer, supplier and employee-specific information (i.e., terms, pricing and compensation) should be held back until you're comfortable the buyer is serious about moving forward with the purchase. We address how to deal with competitors and disclosing sensitive information in *Part III*.

Financial buyers

Financial buyers are generally considered "professional buyers" with a set of investors who finance their transactions. They are typically private equity funds, venture capital funds, buyout funds or private investment funds. Financial buyers tend to buy companies in industries they believe have very strong fundamentals and hold the promise of high returns. They enter and establish a presence in these industries through acquisitions.

As you might guess, the focus of a financial buyer is usually different from a strategic buyer. The financial buyer focuses on the return to their fund (or their investors) they can achieve when they re-sell your company in three-to-seven years (the typical life of a fund). They are very sophisticated and tend to be more creative with structuring the transaction.

Because financial buyers typically are not operating a competing/complementary company, they will not be considering cost savings through consolidation. Their focus will be on profiting from the fundamental strength of the industry in which the company operates. This means they will be concerned primarily about the quality of the management team and the ability of the existing business to capitalize on industry strength and continue growing in the future with outstanding performance.

If you currently wear three hats (primary sales person, CEO <u>and</u> president), a financial buyer might want you and other critical employees to stay involved with the company to ensure a smooth transition of customers, suppliers and employees. This could mean you retain a minority share (less than 50%) of the business or enter into an employment or consulting arrangement. We discuss these arrangements in more detail in *Part III*.

If you have already developed a strong management team and are functioning more as an owner or chairman of the board than a CEO, then your ability to sell and exit without continuing involvement will be stronger. An effective, self-directed management team can be a strong value driver for financial buyers.

Some financial buyers could be considered hybrids of financial and strategic buyers. These financial buyers have already purchased a company in your industry and are looking to acquire and consolidate additional companies to grow revenue and achieve cost savings (like a strategic buyer). You should understand whether you are a platform acquisition (the financial buyer's first in your industry) or whether you will be consolidated into an existing platform company. Their focus will be very different depending on the type of acquisition they are making.

Negotiating with this type of hybrid buyer can be complex, as the buyer is looking at the strategic fit while still focusing on overall returns over a specified period of time (generally much shorter than a strategic buyer's timeline).

> **Expert Insight:**
>
> ### Understand a financial buyer's motivations
>
> When dealing with financial buyers, the first question should be "Is my business your first acquisition in this industry or will my business be consolidated into one of your existing businesses?" Knowing how the buyer plans to run your company after the sale is critical in positioning your business to be a good fit with your buyer's investment requirements. Work with your advisors to understand a financial buyer's motivations before presenting detailed information on your business.

Lifestyle buyers

Lifestyle buyers are typically looking for a business that will support their lifestyle in terms of workload and compensation. They want to be in business for themselves and have decided it's faster to buy a business than build one from the ground up. They're likely a lot like you; maybe even a few years younger.

Lifestyle buyers may be very interested in the quality of your senior management and the predictability of the cash flows from your business. They want a strong team to manage the business on a day-to-day basis and will rely on the cash flows of your business to support their lifestyle.

The risk with these types of buyers is their ability to get funding to buy your business. Financing may be a challenge, and these buyers likely will be relying on cash flows from the business to cover the financing costs as well as to support their lifestyle. You might consider seller financing with these buyers. We discuss the pros and cons of seller financing in *Part III*.

Although the acquisitions can be larger, lifestyle buyers are generally looking at $1 million or less for the purchase price (primarily due to the challenge of getting financing). They are also likely not experienced in buying companies, which might slow down the process. Don't count these buyers out, especially if you own a business valued between $500,000 and $2 million. They may have gone through their own self-discovery process and decided that owning your business is the best fit for what they want out of life or even their next adventure!

Online Resources: Buyers' traits and motivations

Through the *eyes of the buyer*, the potential of your business may look quite different from your own perspective. It is important that you, as the seller, understand your potential buyers. Their traits and motivations will have a direct bearing on how they view your business, and that will play into how they value it. It will also help you focus on the right aspects of preparing your business and maximizing the exit value.

9
How do I estimate the value of my business?

Estimating the value of your business is definitely a worthwhile exercise. It gives you an idea early in the process of what you might be able to achieve in a sale and whether it meets your financial goals at exit. Performing your own valuation may also help you learn more about your business' value drivers and detractors, and how you might enhance its value.

Remember, though, it is the buyer who determines what they will pay based on their objectives, motivation and perspective. Your valuation and the offered price may be very different, especially in the early rounds of negotiation.

So if this is the case, why go through the exercise of estimating the value of your business? Why not just hang a "For Sale by Owner" sign somewhere and then ask interested parties what they would pay? Or, what would be wrong with posting your business on eBay and conducting an online auction to sell it to the highest bidder?

You need to be able to help a buyer see the best in your business and, hopefully, value it as favorably to you as possible. By viewing your business through the *eyes of the buyer* and anticipating the buyer's questions, you will be able to position your business in the most positive light possible and build credibility during the long negotiation process. This can only be done if you have completed a thorough valuation as a starting point.

Three business valuation approaches

There are three primary approaches for estimating the value of a business:

- **Market Approach** – valuation based on multiples from market transactions (sales) of other businesses that are similar to yours ("comparables").
- **Asset Approach** – valuation based on the total of the **fair value** of all **net assets** (assets minus liabilities) controlled by your company.
- **Income Approach** (also called the discounted cash flow approach) – valuation based on today's value of your future cash flows available for use.

Online Resources: Pros and cons of valuation approaches

The valuation of a business can vary significantly based on the perspective of the person doing the work. This is because all of the approaches require inputs, many of which are subjective. A thorough valuation will consider each of these three approaches and determine an overall assessment of value, including a range of potential values. Regardless of the outcome of these three approaches, the final sales price will be based ultimately on *your* exit goals as well as the buyer's valuation.

> **Expert Insight:**
>
> ### Valuation approach versus structure of the sale
>
> The method used to value your business (market, asset or income) does not depend on how you structure the sale of your business. It's important to understand all three valuation approaches so you can make an informed decision on the ultimate value of your business using multiple sources of information. If you are using the asset approach as a valuation method, this does not mean you are planning to structure the sale of your business as an **asset sale** (versus a **stock sale**). The asset approach to valuation is relevant whether you are only selling certain assets or you are selling your entire company. This applies to all valuation approaches.

Why do I think my business is worth more than others do?

In our experience, there is a *fourth approach* to business valuation – the Owner Valuation Approach, or, what the owner perceives the business to be worth. This approach fuels the emotional roller coaster that derails a high percentage of deals and is the primary driver of stress, confusion and frustration for business owners when discussing the value of their business.

There are several reasons that sellers often assign a higher value to their businesses than do potential buyers or advisors:

1. Owners often determine their desired sale price (valuation) based on meeting their financial exit goals (e.g., "I need $2 million to retire, so my business is probably worth $2 million").

2. Owners hear from a variety of "reliable" sources they should get five times earnings or "X" times cash flow based on other transactions.
3. Owners get value in the personal benefits they receive from running their business (flexibility of hours, coverage of everyday expenses, etc.) that a potential buyer may not value.
4. Owners have a deep understanding of their business and how they manage risks, thus, not discounting the value as steeply as might a potential buyer with limited knowledge.
5. Owners attach a sentimental value to their business. Few people recognize the vast amount of time, energy, money and stress that business owners have invested to build their successful business. It has inherent sentimental value to them. It is what leads owners to say, "My business *must* be worth more than that!" Unfortunately, it's difficult to assign an objective dollar figure to sentimental value. It's even more difficult to get buyers to assign *any* value to it.

Market approach to business valuation

The market approach estimates value based on data ("valuation multiples") from similar transactions in the market ("market comparables" or just "market comps"), if any exist. This approach is used more as a data point to check the reasonableness of the valuation calculated under the income approach versus a dollar amount to determine a purchase price.

The market approach tends to reflect underlying fundamentals in your business' sector, but can work either in your favor or against you.

Think back a few years ago to when we faced the housing bubble. Market comps for "plain vanilla" homes took a nosedive as the competition for buyers was fierce and some homeowners had to take low prices just to avoid foreclosure. Conversely, some of the more unique homes in the best locations retained their value, creating market comps that were beneficial to the sellers of these types of homes.

How will market comparables stack up for your business in the Exit Bubble™, where there will be an excess supply of businesses for sale?

- If you operate in a business sector that is appreciating in value due to growth, limited competition, increasing margins, barriers to entry, and other strong fundamentals, you are probably in a seller's market – you're in luck. Market comps for your business should be healthier and the value of your business – and your ultimate sale price – will benefit. In this situation, the market approach of valuation may yield the highest estimate of value for your business.
- If the business sector in which you operate is declining in value due to slowed growth, increased competition, margin compression, low cost of entry, and other problematic fundamentals – you are probably in a buyer's market. You might not be as fortunate with your valuation or sales price using the market approach.

The key to the market approach is to determine the specifics of comparable transactions and then appropriately apply the relevant data to your own business.

For a moment, assume that there are recent transactions for businesses similar to yours, and that you are able to attain access to the specifics of the transactions and the underlying businesses. Let's say you determined that two other businesses similar to yours recently sold for $1 million each. Let's also assume that each business generated cash flows for their owners of $250,000 last year. Now, if your business also generated $250,000 last year for you and it is truly similar to the other businesses, you can feel good about estimating the value of your business at $1 million. Right?

Not exactly. What are the odds you're going to identify an identical company to yours with the exact same cash flows and other risk factors? Not good enough to bet your future on!

The market multiple and to what it is applied (cash flows, in this case) are the critical elements of the approach. The mathematics are straightforward, but the challenges are in attaining the right inputs from appropriate similar businesses.

What's a valid market comp? What's the "right" multiple?

As you may have experienced when buying or selling a home, it can be difficult to use comparables (e.g., $100/square foot) as a valid indicator of value for a specific house. Comparables represent a rule of thumb and are a shortcut to valuing something that may be unique. On the other hand, they may be what the buyer and seller ultimately use to converge on a price acceptable to both. The market approach can lead to trouble if the multiple is not the "right" multiple or if it is applied inappropriately.

You may have colleagues throughout your industry and have heard that they sold their business for a multiple of "X." What you don't know are the nuances behind that multiple, such as the continuing obligations of the seller (e.g., multi-year management contract) or additional investments the buyer intends to make to grow the business. That "X" might be based on cash flows defined differently than you or under different accounting policies than yours. It may even be a multiple of revenues or net income or something other than a multiple of cash flow. Or, that "X" multiple may be associated with a transaction that occurred long ago in a different region for a business not all that similar to yours. To apply that same "X" multiple to your business would be inappropriate in these cases.

Gathering valid and comparable transaction data to apply the market approach can be difficult and is not an exact science. Just consider it a data point in your research to determine the multiplier for your business valuation.

Some might argue that publicly traded companies similar to yours could provide good comps. The problem with using data of publicly traded companies is that those companies may be much larger and more complex than yours, making them not comparable. Furthermore, a private company's equity is not liquid (easily bought and sold) like that of a publicly traded company which translates to easier access to capital. This typically means private companies' values are discounted compared to values of similar public companies.

Market comparables are only a guide

Keep in mind that market comparables should be used only as a guide. Your business may be worth considerably more or less than market comparables based on its consistency of growth and margins, as well as the risks associated with your specific business. For example, variances in value may be due to:

- Factors you can impact, such as quality of management team, inventory controls, accounts receivable or sales/margin growth.
- Factors that you can't easily impact, such as location, tax district, environmental issues, or historic product liability.
- External factors completely outside of your control, such as availability of credit or financing, overall level of private investment in the market, or industry consolidation.

Asset approach to business valuation

The asset approach estimates the value of your business based solely on the current fair value of the assets *and* liabilities of your business. Because this approach does not consider your business' cash flow, growth potential, management talent or other important elements, the resulting valuation could be viewed as a "baseline value." That is, it could be used as a starting point for your lowest possible price.

Why call it the "asset approach" if it also includes liabilities? Even though you'll need to estimate the current *fair* value of your liabilities, there is generally not a significant difference between the *fair* value and **book value** of liabilities. For example, the *fair* value of accounts payable equals the invoice amount, which is the value recorded on your books. Assets that tend to be more tangible, such as land, buildings or equipment, have been depreciated on your books even though they may have appreciated in value in the market.

Example of a net book value calculation:

	Original Cost	Depreciation	Book value	Fair value adjustments	Fair value
Assets:					
Cash	$ 100		$ 100	-	$ 100
Accounts receivable	450		450	-	450
Property, plant & equipment	350	(100)	250	150	400
Other assets	50		50	-	50
	950	(100)	850	150	1,000
Liabilities:					
Accounts payable	(150)		(150)	-	(150)
Debt	(600)		(600)	-	(600)
	(750)	-	(750)	-	(750)
Net book value	$ 200	$ (100)	$ 100	$ 150	$ 250

The asset approach is typically used for asset-intensive businesses such as construction companies with heavy equipment, and heavy manufacturing and real estate companies. It can be used also for struggling companies that have weak earnings and will have to exit by liquidating their assets versus selling the entire company.

> **Expert Insight:**
>
> ### Tax rules to consider
>
> Over the past several years, special tax rules have allowed businesses to accelerate (take more) depreciation on certain assets, resulting in book values substantially lower than fair values of those assets. Using the book value versus the fair value for those assets in the asset approach of valuation may result in an artificially low estimate of your company's value. This could lead you to selling your business at a price lower than necessary. Make sure you identify explicitly for your potential buyers these discrepancies in book value versus fair value to get the full benefit of your assets in your sale price.

Once you determine the *fair* value of your assets and liabilities, you should prepare a table for your potential buyers to adjust the *book* value to *fair* value by each asset type.

> **Online Resources: Asset approach template**

Income approach to business valuation

The income approach of valuation is also referred to as the discounted cash flow approach. This approach is probably the most widely used approach but is also the most complex. There is a perception that the income approach is some kind of mysterious black box of confusing and complex calculations that only an Ivy League MBA can comprehend. While it is true that some buyers have very detailed financial models for analyzing a business, this approach can be tailored to the size and complexity of your business.

> **Expert Insight:**
>
> **More than just a valuation tool**
>
> Not only is the income approach an effective valuation tool in the sale process, it can also provide valuable insights to a business owner regarding value drivers and detractors of their business outside of the sale process. If updated quarterly or annually, this approach can be an effective way to monitor improvements in your business before you exit.

The income approach relies on financial modeling techniques and requires financial input assumptions including a **discount rate**. The income approach attempts to estimate the **present value** (i.e., discounted value) of future cash flows of the business.

The key is estimating future periods' cash flows available to the owner. As tempting as it may be to simply add up all future cash flows to a grand total that serves as your estimate of value, this is not appropriate. Instead, these future years' cash flows need to be converted (or discounted) into terms of today's dollars and then added up to a grand total for valuation.

When discounting cash flows, the further into the future you receive the cash flows, the less they are worth today. Said differently, $1 million in cash flow received five years from now would not be as valuable to you as $1 million today due to general inflation rates and other risk factors over the next five years.

While estimating your business' future cash flows is important, so is establishing the appropriate discount rate or **cost of capital**. An appropriate discount rate is based on the riskiness of your business, relative to other investment opportunities. The riskier your business is, the higher the discount rate should be. The higher the discount rate, the less those future cash flows are worth today. We address the income approach in our online valuation analysis tool.

> **Online Resources: Valuation analysis tool**

We've discussed three different valuation approaches from a technical perspective. Now, it's time to look at how buyers will utilize a valuation to determine what your business is worth to them.

10
What's my business worth?

If you ask five people this question, you will likely get five different answers. You might hear something like, "You should be able to get four maybe five times EBITDA." That sounds like an easy, concise answer, but there is so much more to it. Business valuation is part science and part art, and each person's perspective and approach to valuation can be quite different.

Nonetheless, it's important for business owners to gain an appreciation for their business' value and the process potential buyers will follow to establish their valuation. Having the right financial information ready for your potential buyers will simplify the process for them and will make you a more desirable target in the Exit Bubble™.

> **Expert Insight:**
>
> **Expert Insight: Valuations are estimates**
> One very important rule in the valuation process – the valuation model will give you only an estimate of the value. Don't get locked in on that absolute value. There may be other factors you can't quantify that could materially impact your value. We'll discuss value drivers and detractors in more detail in the next chapter.

How will buyers value my business?

Lifestyle buyers may not be as sophisticated, but strategic buyers and financial buyers will likely lean heavily on the income approach to value your business. They will likely also use elements of the other valuation approaches to refine or validate the income approach.

Normally, buyers use a spreadsheet tool to support the process and apply the income approach. The real power of using a valuation model is that it provides a fast and easy method for a buyer to test how changes in assumptions about your business change its value (i.e., scenario analysis or sensitivity analysis). You, too, will want the ability to run scenario analyses and to understand the sensitivity of your business value to changes in assumptions.

Online Resources: Valuation analysis tool

> **Expert Insight:**
>
> ### What if I don't have time to figure out a valuation analysis tool?
>
> It's okay to have someone assist you in your valuation exercise. In fact, it's highly encouraged. Having said that, don't forget the numbers and assumptions in the model are ultimately your responsibility. You have to be able to support and explain them to a potential buyer. Don't lose credibility with a potential buyer because you aren't able to explain and defend the information in your projections. If you have someone else value your business, make sure you have access to the model or the ability to run scenarios. Staying engaged in the process also helps you identify the value drivers and detractors of your business.

Understanding the general process that most buyers will go through to value your business and calculate their purchase price will help you identify potential value issues that might arise for the buyer. It will also help you objectively review your financial information prior to providing it to a potential buyer.

Interested buyers will generally complete a valuation of your company at least twice during the process:

1. **Initial Valuation**: Calculate an initial value based solely on information provided by the seller to create an offer price for a **letter of intent (LOI)**.
2. **Final Valuation**: Revise initial valuation and offer based on things learned as the buyer really digs into the details of your business (Phase II Diligence).

> **Expert Insight:**
>
> ### Valuation versus worth
>
> You may be happy with your initial valuation calculation and think you're done. Sellers often want to stop here, but buyers are just getting started. Buyers will take that initial valuation and make adjustments for items such as their financing costs, their required return on the investment, and expected transaction costs. Buyers will also make adjustments for real and perceived risks they discover during diligence, including **non-recurring income and expense** items, personal expenses, etc. You must understand and account for these potential adjustments as you consider what your company is worth during the preparation phase.

We dive deeper into the specifics of the actual sale process in *Part III*. For now, let's focus on the general process a buyer might undertake to value a business and calculate an offer price.

Initial valuation
1. Seller gathers historical financial information
2. Seller identifies adjustments to historical financials – **normalizing** and **pro forma**
3. Seller calculates projected cash flows based on pro forma financials and provides to buyer
4. Buyer performs initial valuation based on seller's projections
5. Buyer calculates initial offer for LOI

Final valuation
6. After signing the LOI, buyer confirms seller's normalizing and pro forma adjustments and potentially identifies additional adjustments
7. Buyer revises financial projections based on findings from diligence
8. Buyer performs a final valuation and calculates adjusted purchase price

As you read the steps above, you may notice several references to "adjustments." This is the nature of going through an exit process. The potential for this to occur – a business owner negotiating with a buyer only to have the buyer revise the price downward from the initial price agreed to in the LOI – is called **re-trade risk**.

Once an LOI is in place and you move forward with a potential buyer, it is unlikely that the initial offer will be revised upward. First impressions are key! This is why you must prepare your business before entering the sale process. You need to put the most positive light possible on all aspects of the business from the very beginning to maximize the value and minimize re-trade risk.

Let's break the steps down into a little more detail.

1. Gather historical financial information

For many business owners, gathering historical financial information is easy. They can pull their files or ask their accountant to provide the information. The financial statements should have a professional appearance. Ideally, they should be prepared and presented in accordance with generally accepted accounting principles (GAAP). The financial statements you present to potential buyers will be far more credible if a third party accounting firm has reviewed or audited them.

If you don't have your historical financial information readily available, you should begin to gather it now. It may not come together as quickly or easily as you might hope, but it is the foundation for a quality valuation. You can't expect a potential buyer to guess how your business has performed in the past and offer you a reasonable value.

It's mandatory to have at least one year of historical financial information available for potential buyers. Three years is even better, especially if your business has grown or changed in any material ways in recent years. Buyers will focus on trends or fluctuations over the past few years. They are likely to ask probing questions in these areas, so you should be ready with three years of history if possible. That will help the buyers with their diligence and will build your credibility.

Balance sheet

Potential buyers will use your balance sheet in a number of ways. They will use it as a window into understanding your assets and liabilities and look for signs of value drivers and detractors. **Net working capital** is also of interest to buyers, and it could become part of a final purchase price discussion. This is covered in *Part III*.

Buyers may also use your balance sheet to provide inputs to the asset approach of valuation. If requested, you may need to provide potential buyers with a statement that adjusts the book values on your balance sheet to your estimates of fair values.

Income statement

Potential buyers will be interested in various line items of your income statement and the trends in those items over time (e.g., sales growth rates, gross margin percentage and administrative costs as percentage of sales). What if you had a significant decline in sales two years ago? On the surface, this might scare a potential buyer. If you have already identified the issue and can explain it to the potential buyer, you can minimize the negative impact to the buyer's perception of your business. Identifying those adjustments early will be important for the success of the sale process.

You should calculate your earnings before interest, taxes, depreciation and amortization (**EBITDA**) and **free cash flow (FCF)**. Free cash flow is very similar to EBITDA and is generally defined as cash available to pay yourself a salary and to make payments on your business' debt. EBITDA and FCF will be used throughout the valuation process.

Typically, the buyer will want a full twelve months of EBITDA from which to project future cash flows. This means that if your latest financial statements are as of September 30th, you will need to compile EBITDA for the twelve months ending September 30th, not just for the nine months year-to-date. The term used by most buyers will be trailing twelve months (**TTM**) or last twelve months (**LTM**) EBITDA.

2. Adjust historical financials

"Normalizing" adjustments (quality of earnings exercise)

The buyer will ultimately focus on the quality of your earnings – are they real and repeatable? Buyers will want to know that they can expect to achieve similar or better results if they buy your business. This means you need to go through a detailed process of "scrubbing" your income statement line-by-line and identifying specific expense or income items that a new owner would expect to incur differently or not at all. You will adjust your reported income statement for such items to "normalize" your historical financial statements. This process is often referred to as a **quality of earnings** exercise.

Normalizing adjustments generally fall into two categories: non-recurring and one-time. These items can be expense or income related.

- Non-recurring items could include compensation and benefits of yourself and your family as well as your personal expenses. They represent routine items in the historical financials that are likely to go away after you have exited.
- One-time items could include costs to repair a warehouse after a fire in one year and then the insurance reimbursement for the fire in the next year.

> **Expert Insight:**
>
> **Don't be afraid to talk about "personal" expenses**
>
> In private companies, non-recurring and one-time items, including personal expenses of business owners, are very common. Don't be afraid to identify and disclose them before you sign the LOI while you still have negotiating power with multiple potential buyers.

"Pro forma" adjustments

In addition to normalizing your historical financials for non-recurring and one-time items, you'll want to make pro forma adjustments. "Pro forma" financials assume the transaction occurred as of the beginning of that period, taking into account any changes anticipated in the current business and/or as a direct result of the transaction.

For example, let's assume you know that your health care premiums will increase 15% next year due to a new insurance policy you just signed. You might also assume that a strategic buyer will be consolidating your administrative functions and reducing your operating costs. Given this insight, you would adjust your most recent TTM operating expenses for those potential changes and calculate TTM **pro forma EBITDA**, which will be the starting point for your projected cash flows.

Below is a sample calculation of pro forma EBITDA:

	($ in thousands)
Sales	$ 1,000
Cost of goods sold	(650)
Gross Margin	350
Selling, general and administrative expenses	(100)
Operating Income (loss)	250
Add back non-cash items:	
Interest, taxes, depreciation, amortization	50
EBITDA	300
Adjustments to EBITDA:	
1 Owner's personal expenses	25
2 Increasing health care costs	(10)
3 Annual sales from recently lost customer	(100)
4 Unrecorded liabilities	(2)
5 Bad debt expense	(10)
Pro forma EBITDA	$ 203

The point of Step 2 is to provide a good baseline from which to project future cash flows.

Online Resources: Normalizing and pro forma adjustments

3. Project future cash flows of the business

Adjusting your historical data was setting the stage for building your projections. A solid pro forma income statement creates an excellent base from which to project future results and prepare forward-looking financial statements.

Buyers ultimately will want projections for several years into the future to enter into their valuation model. Business owners often just provide their current year forecast or budget information as projections. This might not work if that information does not reflect the types of adjustments described in Step 2. You should consider the most recent year of your pro forma EBITDA from Step 2 as a reasonable starting point for projections.

Buyers are generally interested in your assumptions of sales growth, gross margin changes, operating expense changes, **capital expenditures** and other cash requirements of the business. While it is only the projected annual free cash flow data that is generally needed for valuation, prudent buyers will want to understand all the details behind your projections. Any projected financials that are markedly different from your historical financials are likely to raise questions. Make sure you can support your projections with solid underlying assumptions or with something more than just "hope."

> **Expert Insight:**
>
> ### Projections - the "optimistic side of realistic"
>
> There are so many things to consider when developing your projections for your business, especially when a third party will be relying on them to determine a purchase price. Although it's important you have facts to support your assumptions, think about creating projections that are on the "optimistic side of realistic." (Make them supportable but on the optimistic side.) A potential buyer will almost always discount a seller's projections, so starting from an optimistic perspective can offset or minimize the effects of that discounting.

4. Calculate initial valuation

You now have the projected cash flows that form the basis of the initial valuation exercise. You'll need to make a number of assumptions in order to estimate how a potential buyer might value your business including:

- Assume a buyer type (financial, strategic, lifestyle)
- Estimate the type of funding (debt, equity, combination) based on buyer type
- Estimate the buyer's cost of the funding to determine the discount rate or **WACC** (weighted average cost of capital)
- Determine the **terminal value** (**TV**)
- Calculate the **present value** (**PV**) of the future cash flows

The items above are the technical piece of valuation and can significantly impact the overall valuation. We've provided definitions for the primary terms in the glossary and more detail on the mechanics of the calculation in our online valuation analysis tool.

How can you make the above assumptions if you don't know who your potential buyer is? Remember, the point of the valuation exercise is not only to come up with a number. It's to identify issues and adjustments early and start to anticipate how they might impact a potential buyer's valuation.

It's likely that potential buyers will perform sensitivity analyses on your financial projections. They also may make explicit adjustments to your projections for certain plans they have for your business. This would especially be the case for strategic buyers who plan to consolidate your operations into their own or financial buyers investing capital to grow your business.

The initial valuation is based on the information you've provided the buyer to date and before the buyer is able to perform diligence on your company. This initial valuation is the basis for the price the buyer will offer in the LOI before diligence begins.

> **Expert Insight:**
>
> ### Why do I care *how* the buyer will pay for my business?
>
> If you're selling your company, why would you care *how* the buyer is paying for your business and what the buyer's weighted average cost of capital is? Wouldn't you simply care that you get paid the amount you want? While you may not have control over the capital structure, it's important to consider the buyer's future financing costs when you value your business. You should also consider the estimated return the potential buyer might require. If you don't make some sort of assumption regarding the components of the buyer's WACC, you could be over-valuing your business. It would also be important to understand the costs of the capital structure if you are retaining any equity in the business, committing to an **earn-out**, or financing a portion of the deal. The future results would be important to you. The valuation analysis tool on **ExitBubble.com** walks you step-by-step through this process.

5. Calculate initial offer for Letter of Intent

After buyers have reviewed the historical, adjusted and pro forma financial information you provided and run it through their valuation model, they will consider whether they remain interested in your business. If they sense a lack of readiness, inconsistent data, questionable commercial performance, or any other factors that concern them, they may discontinue their efforts.

If a potential buyer is still interested, they will wrap up their initial valuation efforts, estimate their transaction costs, and present their initial offer for your business.

When determining their offer price, potential buyers may use the initial valuation amount minus their estimated transaction costs; or, they may shave off a bit more in their offer just to provide a cushion for issues that might be uncovered in diligence. They obviously want to offer you the lowest amount they believe you will entertain. At the same time, they have to consider that other buyers may be aggressive in their offers to you.

Once you receive an LOI, you know the buyer is serious. If all has gone well, you might even have more than one offer. At this point in the process, you will have some decisions to make. We cover those decisions more in *Part III*. For now, let's assume that you have executed an LOI with your chosen potential buyer, and you are ready to move forward.

6. Identify additional adjustments based on diligence

The buyer will now confirm the adjustments you presented to your historical financials and potentially identify new adjustments. We call this Phase II Diligence, which we discuss in more detail in *Part III*.

For example, assume that through diligence efforts, the buyer learns that the long-term lease on your office expires and your rental expenses will jump dramatically next year. If you did not disclose these higher expenses before the LOI, the buyer will make those adjustments and then wonder what else you didn't disclose or overlooked in your projections. This may lead them to dig a little deeper and extend their diligence efforts. By not disclosing the upcoming increase in rental expense up front, you have potentially created a double whammy for yourself.

Hopefully, you've already done a good job of identifying adjustments to your historical financials (both positive and negative). The buyer's goal is to get the best price, not necessarily the "fair" price. If the buyer discovers something favorable during diligence that you didn't include in your projections, they will likely *not* adjust their purchase price upward for that item.

7. Revise financial projections

In addition to finalizing adjustments to your historical financials, the buyer also may make additional adjustments to projections for changes they plan to make to the business after purchasing. For example, a buyer might decide to close a facility or to hire a larger sales force to meet aggressive sales growth targets. Perhaps the buyer will assume an increase in capital injected in the business to support the sales growth. These items can be difficult for the seller to predict. One way to help identify these potential issues is to get to know your buyer and ask questions early in the process. Try to gain as much knowledge as possible about their plans for your business to avoid potential surprises in the final valuation.

8. Calculate final valuation and adjusted purchase price

Once the buyer has finished adjusting historical and projected financials, they will calculate a final valuation of your business and calculate the final purchase price. Hopefully, the buyer has worked closely with you throughout the process, so you have a good understanding of how and why the final offer price has changed from the initial offer in the letter of intent.

Purchase price is one thing, but how much cash will I take home?

In the steps outlined above, you were introduced to items that will affect a buyer's valuation of your business and the offer you might receive. This offer does not equate to the amount of cash you walk away with.

Remember the analogy of selling a house. You never get to pocket 100% of the sales price of a home when you leave the closing table. There are broker fees, closing fees, and paying off the mortgage. Unfortunately, the cash a homeowner gets at closing can be significantly less than the sales price. The same can occur for the sale of a business. When estimating how much cash you can expect to walk away with, you need to account for fees and expenses supporting your sale.

> **Expert Insight:**
>
> ### Don't forget about your costs and debt!
> A common mistake for sellers when figuring out the amount of proceeds they want or need is to forget about their own transaction costs and debt that needs to be paid off at exit. You'll have costs of advisors and you'll need to account for any taxes on the proceeds you might owe at closing and in the future. You may also have debt that needs to be repaid when you sell your business. When determining what amount you want to live on after you exit, don't forget to account for all of these cash outlays!

What if a buyer pays you only part of the purchase price up front and sets up an earn-out for subsequent payments to you? This can complicate matters. Similarly, if the buyer needs you to finance part of the acquisition, then the cash you see at closing is affected.

Example calculation of seller's take home cash

	($ in thousands)
Final purchase price	$ 5,000
Less: Portion deferred in earn-out	(1,000)
Gross proceeds to seller	4,000
Less: Seller's transaction costs	(100)
Less: Seller's debt obligations paid	(300)
Less: Taxes at 20% capital gains rate	(800)
Net cash to seller at closing	**$ 2,800**

There is a long list of all the potential ways that dollars may get squeezed out of your hands as you exit your business. As you start to consider these items, you may get that uneasy feeling in your gut. You start to think about how much cash you really need at exit. You ask yourself, "How low am I willing to go on price before I decide not to sell?"

How low will you go before you walk away?

As we repeatedly emphasize, a business valuation is only an estimate – a starting point for the process of preparing your business for sale and, eventually, a starting point for negotiations with a buyer. Don't get your heart set on a specific value early in the process. There are too many variables that could change that initial value.

We suggest you determine the lowest price you'll accept for your business (**walk-away price**) *before* you begin negotiating with any potential buyers. Many sellers wait until they are in final price negotiations before they think about their walk-away price. At that point, exhaustion and stress have taken their toll and your emotions are running high. Clearly, this is the wrong state of mind in which to make such a significant decision.

Consider this story: We know a business owner, Joe, who agreed to a price in a LOI and assumed the buyer's diligence process would have little impact on that price. When signing the LOI, the buyer assumed his existing operations would consolidate into Joe's facilities, saving rent on the buyer's existing facilities. Upon further review, engineers decided the configuration of Joe's facilities would not allow for consolidation. The buyer reduced his offer price in the 11th hour of negotiations. Joe was unprepared for this last-minute reduction in price and hadn't taken the time early in the process to figure out the lowest price he would accept. He was exhausted from the process and just wanted to be done. He accepted the lower price and soon found himself looking for a job to support his family. Joe had to find a way to earn it again because he hadn't determined his walk-away price before entering into negotiations. Looking back, selling may not have been the best exit strategy for Joe at that time.

Once you've established your walk-away price, compare it to your estimated business value to understand how far you might want or need to "move the needle" on the value of your business prior to selling it. If your estimated business value less your transaction costs is equal to or greater than your walk-away price, you may decide to sell your business sooner than if you don't think you can meet or beat your walk-away price.

Now that we've discussed adjustments to your estimated business value and your walk-away price, let's talk about additional adjustments to your company's value that may be more difficult to quantify, but can be even bigger issues than the adjustments we discussed above.

11
What is my "Value Profile"?

In the previous chapters, you learned about basic valuation techniques, how a potential buyer might arrive at a purchase price, and how that purchase price might translate into cash for the seller. Now it's time to understand what other factors could impact the value of your business, although they may be difficult to quantify. You will want to identify the value drivers and value detractors of your business in your "Value Profile."

A Value Profile is a tool that we developed to assist sellers in identifying value drivers and detractors of their businesses. A summarized version of the Value Profile is *included free when you access your online* Book Level Membership of ExitBubble.com. The *comprehensive*, interactive Value Profile tool is included as part of the valuation analysis tool for Exit Bubble Elite.

Value drivers and detractors

During the sale process, buyers will identify factors that drive and detract from the value of your business based on industry comparables, their prior experiences, or their plans for the business going forward. These value drivers and detractors can often be the items that make or break a deal.

Identifying value drivers and detractors through the *eyes of the buyer* is a critical part of preparing your business for exit. You'll want to prepare an action plan to address the detractors in order to increase the sale value of your business. How do you determine what is a driver and a detractor in the *eyes of the buyer*? Take these examples:

- 40% of your sales are concentrated in one customer that you've had for 20 years. You may see this fact as a driver of value because it's such a long, stable customer relationship. The buyer sees this as a value detractor because, if you lose this customer, 40% of your business is gone.
- You've built a very strong brand for the company that centers around you, as the owner and lead sales rep. You see your strong brand as a driver of value. A buyer sees this as a value detractor because there's a risk that the value of the brand will walk out the door with you at exit.

As you can see from the two simple examples above, your perception of what drives value can be very different from the buyer.

How do you begin to identify your drivers and detractors through the *eyes of the buyer*? Below is a sample of some high-level questions about your business, industry and the general market a buyer might consider when identifying value drivers and detractors.

- Are your cash flows predictable?
- Are your earnings real and repeatable?
- What is the quality of your management team?
- Is your industry expanding or contracting?
- What barriers to entry exist?
- Is the regulatory environment getting more or less restrictive?

Online Resources: Value Profile worksheet

As the owner of your business, you have lived in this environment for your entire career. You intuitively know and understand the workings of your business – the risks, customer nuances, processes and procedures, etc. The potential buyers will need to question and understand every aspect of your business using their own perception of value drivers and detractors.

> **Expert Insight:**
>
> **Not all buyers are experts**
>
> You may be surprised to find that many potential buyers will be completely new to your particular business sector or niche. This is especially true with lifestyle buyers. Their lack of knowledge of your business may cause these buyers to discount value for perceived risks that you don't view as risks. This is why it's important to understand who your potential buyers might be and view your business through their eyes to address risks they might identify. Be prepared to educate your potential buyer on value drivers and how you view and manage potential value detractors.

In developing your Value Profile, you'll want to dive into the specifics of your business, including sales, operations, human resources, financial, legal, and technology to get a more in-depth understanding of your drivers and detractors. A good **information request list** (**IRL**) will give you a comprehensive list of the most commonly requested information in each of these areas from potential buyers. This list is also often referred to as a diligence checklist or data request list.

Online Resources: Sample information request list

Why look at this checklist *before* you decide to sell your business? Looking at the information buyers will request and anticipating their questions will help you identify your value drivers and detractors early enough to either correct them or prepare to address them during the diligence process. While many of these items may not seem relevant to you or your business, a buyer may be interested in why you feel that way. You should be prepared to articulate both the why's and why not's, if asked.

How valuable is your management team?

When was the last time you objectively assessed how key members of your management team were performing, and whether they would be willing to remain with the company under a new owner? Most sellers don't have or take the time to really assess their management team through the *eyes of the buyer*, even though it is critical to preparing your business for exit. As a team, your management group is likely quite effective. Weaknesses in one member are probably overcome by another, and the job gets done. So why worry?

When a buyer is looking at your management team, they don't have the history and personal relationships with your team that you have. The buyer will likely not be as forgiving and only want people who are clearly capable of taking the company to the next level with a new owner. This ultimately can create an unfortunate situation for the under-performing employee, but it also may increase your stress level and decrease the value you receive for your business.

In *Part I*, we discuss how you might determine whether the business could run without you by being able to take extended vacations with little disruption to the business. That scenario is a good indication of the strength of your management team. Are they capable of running the business without you? If yes, that could be a value driver for a potential buyer.

The importance of this potential value driver will differ depending on the potential buyer's plans for the business after purchasing. The quality of your management team could be more valuable to a financial buyer who needs the existing team to continue running the business versus a strategic buyer who plans to consolidate your operations into their existing operations and already has a strong management team.

Some believe the management team is an intangible value of a business and difficult to quantify. Others believe it's very tangible and will quantify the cost of (1) replacing certain management who decide not to stay with the new owner or (2) hiring a more qualified person. As you can see, for a seller, it can be difficult to put a value on a management team for a potential buyer.

Regardless of who your buyer might be and how they might value your management team, performing an assessment on your management team can help you work better with your team and improve their performance while you're still running your business. If you're unsure how to assess your team, consider using an outside resource to help you objectively assess your management team without personal or professional bias.

What about the intangible value of my business?

The **intangible value** of your business relates to the value of assets that can't be seen or touched, but still have value to you and, more importantly, to a potential buyer. Some of these assets can be valued and recorded on the books, such as capitalized software, but more often than not there is no value on your books for these types of assets. **Goodwill** is often incorrectly used interchangeably with the term intangible value. However, goodwill is the amount a buyer will pay for a business over the value of the tangible assets of a business. In an acquisition, the buyer will record goodwill as an intangible asset. The Value Profile tool should help you identify potential intangible assets of your business.

Here are a few examples of intangible assets you might consider in your business and a buyer might value:

- Customer lists
- Strong, tenured employees
- Significant backlog of orders
- High brand recognition
- Patents or trademarks
- Unique location
- Exclusive distribution arrangements
- Favorable lease

These intangible assets might be the distinguishing factor between your business and another seller's business. They could also serve as a nice offset to value detractors in negotiations with the buyer. For a seller, it's difficult to put an actual dollar value on these assets because the value will be different for each potential buyer. Make a list of potential intangible assets of your business so you are prepared to discuss these with your advisors and with potential buyers as they begin asking questions. Being proactive by helping potential buyers identify intangible value may increase their overall valuation of your business.

Discounting your estimated business value for the "great unknown"

You've already identified normalizing adjustments to your financial statements and considered adjustments for potential value drivers and detractors, including intangible assets. What other adjustments should you be concerned about?

There's always a chance that something unexpected will come up during the buyer's diligence process. These unexpected items often result in the buyer discounting or "re-trading" the price you already agreed to in the LOI. We discuss re-trade risk in more detail in *Part III*.

These unknown items could be buyer-specific and depend on a variety of factors, including the buyer's plans for the company after the sale. It's difficult to predict the exact nature and impact of all risks uncovered during the diligence process. To be safe, we recommend you apply an additional discount to your estimated business value as a cushion for the unknown.

There's no good rule of thumb for what this cushion should be. You should consider the complexity of your business and the likelihood of a buyer discovering an issue during diligence and re-trading the offer price. You should also consider how much cushion you believe there currently is between an estimated price and your walk-away price. This is effectively your safety net against the unknown.

Now that you've identified the value drivers and detractors of your business, it's time to make some critical decisions on whether and how you want to address those drivers and detractors prior to exiting.

12
When do I pull the trigger on my exit?

After you've estimated your business value and identified your value drivers and detractors, you'll want to take a step back and revisit your exit options again. What do you want to accomplish and when do you want to accomplish it?

If, after revisiting your exit options, you select the option to sell, you'll want to go through a series of questions/steps to determine *when* you want to put your business on the market for sale. As the popular saying goes, "Timing is everything."

The first question you ask yourself compares your estimated business value to your walk-away price. We'll start with the right side of the decision tree on the next page.

If the estimated business value meets or exceeds your walk-away price, do you want to make improvements to your business that might increase the value of your business above your walk-away price?

Remember, your walk-away price is the *lowest* price you are willing to take. You may decide you'd like to make some improvements to your business that would increase the potential value of your business above that price.

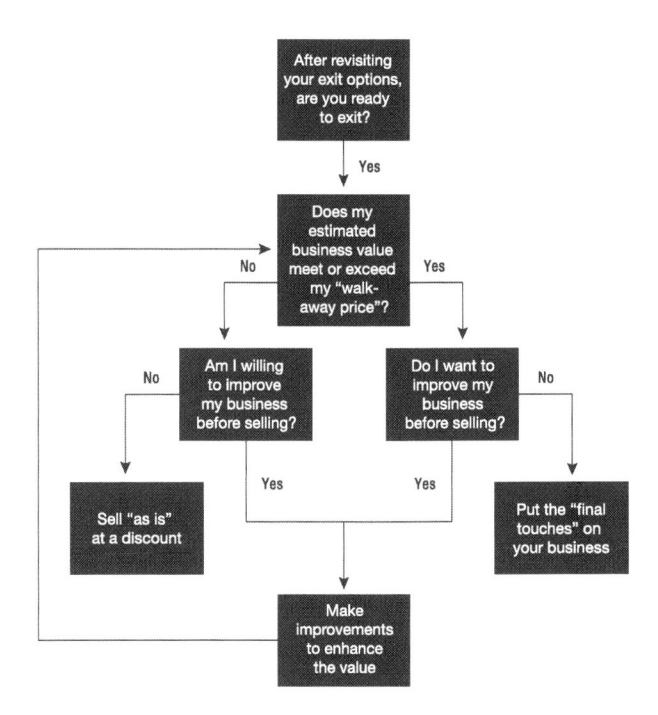

```
                    ┌─────────────────┐
                    │ After revisiting│
                    │ your exit options,│
                    │  are you ready  │
                    │    to exit?     │
                    └────────┬────────┘
                             │ Yes
                             ▼
                    ┌─────────────────┐
                    │    Does my      │
                    │   estimated     │
          ┌─── No ──│ business value  │── Yes ──┐
          │         │ meet or exceed  │         │
          │         │    my "walk-    │         │
          │         │   away price"?  │         │
          │         └─────────────────┘         │
          │                                     │
          ▼                                     ▼
  ┌──────────────┐                    ┌──────────────┐
  │ Am I willing │                    │ Do I want to │
  │  to improve  │── No ──┐   ┌── No ─│  improve my  │
  │ my business  │        │   │       │   business   │
  │before selling?│       │   │       │before selling?│
  └──────┬───────┘        │   │       └──────┬───────┘
         │ Yes            │   │              │ Yes
         │                ▼   │              │
         │         ┌──────────────┐          │
         │         │ Sell "as is" │          │
         │         │ at a discount│          │
         │         └──────────────┘          │
         │                                   │
         │         ┌──────────────┐          │
         │         │Put the "final"│         │
         │         │  touches" on │          │
         │         │ your business│          │
         │         └──────────────┘          │
         ▼                                   ▼
              ┌─────────────────┐
              │      Make       │
              │   improvements  │
              │   to enhance    │
              │    the value    │
              └─────────────────┘
```

For example, you may have identified the high level of your selling, general and administrative (**SG&A**) expenses as a potential value detractor. After discounting for the high level of expenses, you still believe you could meet or exceed your walk-away price. You might decide, however, that you could make some cost reductions over the next two years (e.g., travel and entertainment, insurance contracts, and miscellaneous expenses) resulting in an estimated 20% increase in your valuation. Is that additional 20% achievable? Do you have the time and energy to make it happen, or would you be happy with the lower price?

These are difficult questions for sellers. You always want the highest possible price for your life's work, but the cost of improving your business (financially and emotionally) can sometimes outweigh the ultimate benefit.

You should also consider if you've prepared yourself for the exit. If you haven't, this may tip the scales toward making the improvements over the next two years to give you and your business more time to prepare for the exit. Once you've made improvements and you and your business are ready, it's time for some important "final touches."

If the estimated value meets or exceeds your walk-away price but you don't want to make any improvements to your business in hopes of achieving a higher valuation, then you would move straight to the "final touches." What does this mean?

Instead of making improvements, putting the final touches on your business is more cosmetic with the hope of appealing to potential buyers. For example, in a house, you would clean out the closets, shampoo the rugs, plant some flowers, and maybe bake some cookies so the house smells inviting. For a business, you might get your corporate documents in order, hire an outside accountant to prepare professional-looking financial statements, and clean and organize your offices and facilities.

Let's move to the left side of the decision tree. If the estimated business value does not meet or exceed your walk-away price, you have to ask yourself if you want to sell your business "as is" at a potentially low price. Or, do you want to make improvements to your business that might increase the value of your business to at least exceed your walk-away price?

You might be too tired to spend time making improvements to the business. Using the housing analogy, you may know that you need new paint, the deck needs repair, and the kitchen needs to be updated. However, you'd rather take a lower price now than spend the time and effort to make those repairs before you sell it.

Even though the goal of beating the Exit Bubble™ is to make sure you don't have to earn it again, you may decide it's more important to get out of your business now. Maybe you simply don't enjoy it anymore and would be happy working for someone else in a less stressful job and spending more time with your family.

Selling now "as is" is always an option. Make sure you understand the impact to your post-exit income and are prepared to either down-shift in retirement or find another stream of income to support you and your family. If you decide on this path for exit, make sure you've also prepared yourself for life after the sale before entering the sale process. We discuss this in more detail in *Part I*.

> ### Gut Check: I'm burned out and want out of my business
>
> If you find yourself in this position, take a deep breath and consider your options. If you continue through the sale process, the buyer might sense your state of mind and you might end up taking a much lower price than what your business is worth, simply because you're tired. Maybe selling at this time isn't your best option. Creating or hiring a second-in-command to take on the bulk of the work and continue to improve the business may be a good option for you. Bottom line, try to make this decision before you're emotionally spent or burned out.

This decision tree is a simplified example of what to consider when determine the timing of your exit. You'll want to discuss these decision points in great detail with your family, advisors, and possibly some of your management team when the time is right. You'll also want to be prepared to take advantage of a market peak and exit possibly before you've finished preparing your business.

If you decide you want to spend time improving the value of your business, you need to create and implement your action plan for improvement.

13
How do I improve my Value Profile?

After you develop a fairly comprehensive list of potential drivers and detractors of your business as discussed in Chapter 11, it's time to create an action plan to correct or minimize the impact of the detractors. You might be asking yourself, "How do I know what to improve?"

Consider the story of someone preparing their house for sale and replacing old orange shag carpet with new orange shag carpet. In the seller's eyes, they've increased the value of their home because the carpet is new. In the *eyes of the buyer*, the investment in new orange shag carpet hasn't improved the value of the home and may have reduced the number of potential buyers. In fact, some buyers might wonder what other bad decisions will be costly to correct after they move in.

In order to avoid wasting valuable time and money and potentially creating more issues for potential buyers, create an action plan to address your value detractors.

1. Prioritize your value detractors based on impact to your business value
2. Determine cost/benefit of "fixing" or addressing each detractor
3. Get buy-in from your team

Prioritize your value detractors

We generally classify value detractors into three categories:

- *Deep wounds* – Buyer might be scared away quickly or go through diligence and severely discount the value (e.g., environmental liability).
- *Flesh wounds* – Buyer might decide the "wound" can be healed but will discount the value of the business for the effort to fix (e.g., implement a new IT system).
- *Cosmetic* – Might attract more buyers initially, but might not directly impact the ultimate valuation of your business (e.g., audited financial statements).

You might need help from your advisors or management team to determine how to categorize each detractor. Remember, you're always looking at detractors through the *eyes of the buyer*. You'll need to take into account the different types of buyers who might be interested in your business and their perspectives on the detractors.

For example, if you think your business would be a good fit for a strategic buyer who is currently a competitor, then having a lower performing management team might not be an issue as the buyer may already have a talented management team who could run the combined companies.

Determine the cost/benefit of "fixing" your value detractors

Next, look at the probability of being able to "fix" the issue and the cost/benefit of doing so before you enter the sale process. Remember your decision tree exercise in the last chapter. You may not want or be able to fix all potential detractors, so you'll need to prioritize your efforts on the ones that will yield the most value for the effort.

> **Expert Insight:**
>
> **The real cost of fixing a value detractor**
>
> When determining the cost/benefit of fixing a value detractor, consider available resources, time, effort and, most importantly, cost. Cost is measured not only in dollars, but also by the amount of effort it will take from you and your team and the distractions from running your business.

Let's look at an example assuming your buyer is a financial buyer. You perform a management assessment and determine you don't have a logical second-in-command who could run the company for a new owner after you exit (a potential value detractor for a financial or lifestyle buyer). You could hire and train someone to take on that role, but you determine this option would be cost-prohibitive. You also don't feel like you have the time to train someone <u>and</u> do your own job. You decide not to hire anyone.

When you're ready to discuss this issue with a potential financial buyer, you might focus on the following:

- You recognize that there is no logical second-in-command who could run the company for the buyer after you exit.
- You performed an analysis and the cost and effort of bringing someone new into the company <u>prior to your exit</u> didn't make good financial sense for you.
- During the analysis, you wrote a detailed job description and skill sets you believe are important for that position and can share that with the buyer.

- You also have a list of potential candidates you researched before you decided not to move forward with the hire.
- You may also consider signing an employment contract to stay for a period of time to train a new CEO.

You've demonstrated that you can identify a value detractor, analyze your options, and have a meaningful discussion of potential options for the buyer after the sale. This gives the buyer comfort that your business has been well run.

When determining the cost/benefit of addressing value detractors, consider the following questions:

- Is this an issue that can be fixed?
- What's the probability it can be fixed?
- What will it cost to fix?
- How long do you estimate it will take to fix?
- Do you have the people to fix it?
- Do you have the energy to fix it?
- If you fix it, by how much will it improve valuation or attract more buyers?
- If you don't fix it, is it a deal killer or can you effectively address it with a potential buyer?
- Would you rather risk a potential price discount than go through the effort of fixing the issue(s)?

The "people" aspect of your action plan to fix detractors is the most critical piece. You can't do it all by yourself. Even if you could, you don't have the time and you can't afford to let your existing business suffer during the process. If you don't have buy-in from your team, you're likely not going to be successful.

Balancing management buy-in with confidentiality

How do I get buy-in from my management team on the action plan if I'm not ready to disclose my exit plans? This is a common question, and one that can be quite tricky. Your answer may be impacted by the time frame in which you expect to exit. If it's more than two years, then it's logical what you're doing is simply improving your business. You can honestly frame the discussion with your team that way. If it's a shorter time frame or the action items signal that you might be exiting, then you may need to put your communication plan in place earlier than expected. We discuss communication planning in Chapter 16.

Only you know your management team and how to motivate them to embrace the action plan. Remember, preparing your business for exit is really about increasing the value of your business. That should be a goal for you and your management team regardless of your exit plans.

> **Expert Insight:**
>
> ### Continue to keep your options open
>
> Identifying and addressing value detractors are not solely for the purpose of preparing your business for exit. As a business owner, your goal should always be to improve your business and maximize the number of personal and professional options available to you. You may decide, after implementing an action plan to improve your business, you'd rather stay involved with the business as an "owner/chairman" instead of the CEO/president. This might meet both your financial needs and your desire to spend more time outside of the company. Keep your mind and options open!

Once you've prioritized the value detractors, determined the cost/benefit of fixing those issues and achieved buy-in from your team, it's time to actually create your action plan.

Creating an action plan

You've completed the difficult task of identifying your issues and determining the resources required. Now, you need to create action steps to address the value detractors and assign responsibility to your team.

There are numerous resources available online for action plan templates and other project management tools. We recommend you keep it as simple as possible. If it's too complicated or takes too much time to maintain, your team will likely not use it. Based on the nature and complexity of your individual action items, you will need to assess how detailed and complex your tracking system or project management tool needs to be.

Online Resources: Action plan template

Some important rules to remember when creating an action plan:

- Define actions that are specific and measurable. The goal of "increasing sales" is not effective. The goal of "increasing sales of Product X by 10% by June 30th" is specific and measurable.
- List actions in order of highest to lowest priority.
- Create a deadline for completing each action. If there's no deadline, it will never get done.
- Assign a primary person responsible for completing each action step who will update progress throughout the project.

- Color-code status of completing the action using yellow (on track) and red (at risk for achieving). For completed items, move to bottom of template and shade it gray.

There are entire books written on effective project management. Everyone has his or her preferred method. What's most important is that you create a plan that can be followed and easily maintained by everyone on your team.

> **Expert Insight:**
>
> ### An increase in profits doesn't guarantee an increase in value
>
> As you're preparing your business for exit and looking at areas where you can improve performance, make sure you're considering how it will potentially impact the value of your business to the next owner. For example, you might own a business that makes lamp stands. In order to grow top line revenue and profits, you decide to buy a lamp shade business. On the surface, this would seem to make your business more valuable – you've increased your product offerings and profits. However, what if the implied market value for lamp stands was ten times EBITDA and lamp shades was only two times EBITDA? You've now potentially decreased the overall value of your business when you exit. Consider how your growth plans will impact your value to a future buyer of your business.

14

How do I implement and track my plan?

You've identified and prioritized your value drivers and detractors and your team has bought in to the action plan. That's progress, but just knowing what needs to be improved does not solve the issues. As Vince Lombardi said, "Hope is not a strategy." You must put together a strategy to implement your plan and monitor your progress against your plan. If you can't measure your success, how will you manage it or know when you've achieved it?

We encourage you to create a "dashboard" of the key metrics that you'll be tracking to determine progress on the action plan. A dashboard is simply a one-page summary that tracks your key metrics or key performance indicators (**KPIs**). Each dashboard is customized to your business and the KPIs you want to track.

For example, if you have an action step to improve your accounts receivable collection from 50 to 30 days within twelve months, you would include on your dashboard how many days your receivables are outstanding each period, so you could monitor progress to meeting that goal.

Best practice is to establish KPIs at more detailed levels than overall the company results (e.g., by department, product/service, division, location).

Given how busy you and your team will be, a dashboard is an effective way to communicate progress and maintain focus on the action plan.

How do I determine which metrics to use on my dashboard?

This can be a complicated matter. One type of business might track revenues per employee, while another might track average sales per customer. There are some resources for smaller companies that provide "rule of thumb" operating metrics. For example, *The Business Reference Guide – the Essential Guide to Pricing Businesses and Franchises (Tom West, 2013)* might be a good starting point for understanding some general industry metrics that would be relevant for your type of business. Potential buyers will also be comparing you to industry metrics they've researched.

Rules of thumb are helpful in a general sense, but you just went through a fairly significant and detailed process to determine your value drivers and detractors. Use that process to flush out the KPIs that are most relevant to *your* business and your identified value drivers and detractors.

> **Expert Insight:**
>
> ### Don't forget about your value drivers
> Often when you're so focused on your value detractors, you can lose focus on what you do well. Don't take your eye off of your value drivers and allow them to suddenly become detractors! Identifying appropriate metrics to monitor value drivers and including them on your dashboard will keep them in focus for you and your team.

Get credit for the improvements you make

One of the great uses of the action plan and dashboard is to show a potential buyer how you and your team have improved the business. Be prepared to discuss in detail what changes have been implemented in your business to improve operations and address the value detractors that you identified.

During diligence, you should be able to pull out your monthly dashboards and discuss with a potential buyer how you and your team addressed your issues. Tie the results to specific items in your action plan and explain how they improved your earnings or cash flows. Show the cause and effect. This will give you and your team instant credibility and put a more positive spin on detractors that may negatively impact your historical financials.

> **Gut Check: Do I really want to sell?**
> At this point, you may have spent considerable time and effort identifying and addressing your value drivers and detractors. In doing so, you may find that your business is running better than ever and your management team is firing on all cylinders. Revisit your exit options from Part I and ask yourself the following:
> - Now that my business is running smoothly, do I really want to exit?
> - Would I rather move into a "chairman" position, allow my management team to run the day-to-day operations, and spend more time outside of the business?
> - Should I consider an ESOP or management buyout to allow my employees to buy the business?
> - Am I re-energized by the improvements made and want to continue working a little while longer?
> - Am I ready to sell the business?
>
> Make sure you allow yourself to revisit your options throughout your exit planning process.

So far in *Part II*, we've focused on valuing your business and how to impact that value. Now, we'll discuss the importance of advisors and developing communication plans. Don't move forward without engaging the right advisors and having a communication plan in place.

15
Do I really need advisors? (Yes!)

In *Part I*, we discuss getting your financial advisor or CPA involved early in your exit planning as they can play a vital role in helping you determine your financial needs after you exit your business. In this chapter, you'll learn the role and responsibilities of <u>all</u> potential advisors you might want to engage and how best to engage them.

You may be saying to yourself, "I already know a business broker from my monthly trade association meeting," or, "I trust the CPA I've used for my tax returns for 20 years." These are valuable relationships with people who may be very competent in their fields. We challenge you to consider whether these advisors have the right skills for <u>your transaction</u>. How many transactions has the business broker completed in your industry and what size were the businesses? How many sale transactions has your CPA worked on in the past couple of years, if ever?

> **Expert Insight:**
>
> **Take time to interview potential advisors**
>
> Selecting advisors is a critical part of the sale process. For example, a dentist is a doctor, but you wouldn't want your dentist to pull your tonsils, would you? This is not the time to employ friends or acquaintances because it's the easiest option, nor is it the time to try to learn these roles and take them on yourself. Take the time to interview advisors and select the best ones for your transaction.

Advisors are critical to a successful process. An important step in deciding which advisors to engage is to understand fully the roles and responsibilities of each type of advisor prior to engaging them. By knowing what each advisor contributes to the exit process, you can determine which advisors are appropriate for you and when and how to bring them in. It also makes it easier to ask questions so you select the best advisor for your needs.

Advisor	Primary Role
Financial Advisor	Plan your post-exit financial needs
CPA/Accountant	Understand tax implications of various structures and prepare or audit financial statements for diligence, if needed
Attorney	Structure and prepare the transaction documents; estate and tax planning
Business Broker	Coordination of all parties involved, sourcing a buyer and negotiating the transaction; generally for companies less than $5 million
Investment Banker	Same as a business broker; generally for companies greater than $5 million

Online Resources: Advisors' roles and responsibilities

Often, one advisor can serve multiple roles in an exit process. For example, your attorney may be a CPA and can assist with tax matters. That attorney may also be an experienced transaction attorney who can help with activities a business broker would normally perform, like sourcing buyers and negotiating the transaction, if your company is small and not complex. A note of caution: We believe the only time it's appropriate not to consider engaging a business broker or investment banker is if your company is small and your business is not complex. Even then, you should consider whether you and your other advisor(s) are capable of taking on the responsibilities of a business broker while running your business and performing other duties. Business brokers generally get paid a small retainer fee up front, then a success fee (i.e., a percentage of the proceeds). If your company doesn't sell, then you don't incur additional costs.

You might be a smaller business and considering selling your company through alternative channels, such as online auction sites like BizBuySell.com, BizQuest.com, or BusinessMart.com. In that case, you will likely still want a CPA/financial advisor to help you understand your financial requirements after exiting and tax implications of the structure, as well as a lawyer who can help review your sale documents.

Although, the size of your business can impact whether you hire a business broker or an investment banker, the amounts discussed above are only general ranges. Some business brokers will work on larger transactions and some investment bankers will work on smaller transactions. Even if you believe you're too small to hire a business broker, we encourage you to at least talk to them and get their views on your business and current market conditions for selling a business. The more information you have, the better prepared you'll be.

Experienced business brokers and investment bankers can make the difference between getting your business sold at the greatest possible value and failing in your exit attempt. An experienced broker or investment banker can allow you to continue running your business while going through the lengthy sale process. We discuss how time-consuming the sale process can be in *Part III*.

How do I find the right advisors?

An important part of the selection process is to know what interview questions to ask potential advisors. Some general questions are as follows:

- How many years have you been an advisor?
- How many transactions have you successfully completed in the past three years?
- Are you knowledgeable about my industry and have you done transactions in my industry?
- May I call on your previous clients for references?
- How is your fee structured?
- How do you source potential buyers?

> **Expert Insight:**
>
> ### Beware of the "guaranteed sale"
>
> Don't start seeing dollar signs and fall into the trap of unrealistic promises from your advisors regarding how quickly they can sell your company and at what valuation. We've all heard the stories about the owner down the street who sold his business in three months at a multiple of five times earnings. But is that really true? If it is, that doesn't mean you'll have the same experience. Each transaction is different and has its own unique challenges. Be suspect of the advisor who guarantees a sale within a short period of time or guarantees a high multiple. There are no guarantees in the exit process, other than it won't go smoothly if you aren't prepared. Hire experienced advisors and keep your expectations realistic.

You'll be asking many questions of your potential advisors, but it's equally important to listen to the questions they ask you. Do they want to get to know your company in detail, or are they willing to represent you with only a high-level understanding? Are they asking detailed questions about all aspects of your business, including your reason for selling? Are they interested in the quality of your management team? They should be asking just as many questions of you as you are of them during the selection process. If your advisor is not fully engaged and interested, you, your team and your business likely will not have a good experience with them.

> **Expert Insight:**
>
> ### Protect your information during the advisor selection process
>
> In selecting the right transaction advisors, you may need to share a fair amount of information about your business and exit plans with several candidates. Don't forget to have the candidates sign a **nondisclosure agreement (NDA)** before you share any information. If you decide not the engage them, you don't want them disclosing your potential exit plans to anyone. While most advisors are very professional, better to be safe than sorry when dealing with confidentiality.

Selecting a business broker or investment banker

The questions to ask financial advisors, attorneys and CPAs are fairly straightforward and easy to understand. If you've not worked with a business broker or investment banker before, you might need a little more information on their approach to marketing your company before you start interviewing. There are pros and cons with the "wide net" and targeted marketing approaches business brokers and investment bankers generally take to source potential buyers.

"Wide net" marketing approach

Using the wide net approach, your advisor sends a summary of your company to hundreds of potential buyers based on your advisor's contact list. The advisor doesn't qualify the potential buyers ahead of time. In these cases, your company summary could be combined with several other summaries and sent as a package. This approach is most common for companies on the smaller end of the spectrum. Listing your business anonymously on an internet site would fall into this category too.

- Pro: Your company reaches the largest number of potential buyers.
- Con: Your company could get lost among the other companies in the package. Also, you may waste time wading through bidders who may not be serious buyers.

Targeted marketing approach

The targeted marketing approach requires your advisor to research potential buyers ahead of time to identify those who might be interested in your company (size, industry, ability to execute, etc.). Your company information is only sent to the pre-qualified list of buyers.

- Pro: Doesn't waste you and your advisor's time dealing with bidders who aren't serious buyers and may result in better quality bids.
- Con: Takes more time on the front end as the advisor qualifies the list.

> **Expert Insight:**
>
> **Control who sees your company's information**
> Regardless of the approach used to communicate with potential buyers, we strongly recommend you review the list of potential buyers before any communication is sent. You want to be sure your competitors, suppliers or customers aren't receiving information you don't want them to have at this stage of the process.

Fee structures

Business brokers and investment bankers use a variety of fee structures. You'll want to understand the structure your advisor is proposing for the exact services to be provided. Assess whether you believe the amount of time and effort is worth the fee they are likely to collect. You won't feel good about paying an advisor a huge fee if you don't feel like they supported it with good value. At the same time, you want your advisor incented appropriately to work hard for you in helping you achieve your successful exit.

The most common pricing structure is the declining percentage method, a success fee based on the sales price.

Below is an example of how a fee might be structured based on a total purchase price of $5 million.

- Agreed upon initial retainer to be applied to final commission
- 10% of the first $1 million of selling price
- 8% of the second $1 million
- 6% of the third $1 million
- 4% for anything over $3 million

Depending on the actual sales price and the effort expected by the advisor to sell your company, the buckets and percentages can vary dramatically. Nonetheless, the theory is the same. Generally, the higher the sales price, the lower the overall percentage earned on that sales price.

Another option may be to pay an advisor a monthly retainer. When the sale occurs, the fees paid to the advisor would be reduced by what you'd already paid in retainer fees. This structure obviously favors the advisor as they are paid some amount even if your company never sells.

Another alternative is an hourly arrangement for more limited involvement, such as help identifying potential buyers and a review of your materials.

There's no right or wrong way to structure a fee arrangement. A good rule of thumb is that the larger and more complex your business, the more time and effort an advisor will spend in the marketing process.

> **Expert Insight:**
>
> ### It's important to like your advisors
>
> Although qualifications and past deal experience are important, it's equally as important to trust and like your advisors. You will be working with them during an intense and emotional time for you and your employees. Your advisors become part of your team and your business through this process. Get to know them and be thoughtful and thorough in your selection process.

Online Resources: Background checks on advisors

16
How do I control communication?

Scenario 1: Your largest customer calls you one day and, after chatting about yesterday's game, suddenly asks, "I heard you're selling the company. Is that true?" Given you haven't told anyone about your plans to sell, this catches you off guard. You don't want to lie because the sale will eventually become public knowledge. On the other hand, you still want to keep it confidential. You can't risk losing your largest customer. What do you do?

Scenario 2: Your top sales person walks into your office and says, "There are rumors you're selling the company. Is it true? How will this impact me?" You're still in the early stage of deciding how to proceed with the sale process and you haven't discussed it with your management team. Just like your largest customer, you can't afford to lose your top sales person. How do you respond?

Scenarios like these could happen at some point in the process. Keeping deals confidential is almost impossible the longer the process continues. You have to be ready with your responses to questions like these and make them consistent every step of the way.

Scenario 3: You are having dinner with a potential buyer and the evening has gone smoothly. You've talked about the strength of your business and employees and the opportunities for growth, and the buyer seems completely engaged in the conversation. You're thinking, "This is going just as I had planned - this buyer will want to buy my company for exactly what I'm asking." During dessert, the buyer asks a simple question, *"It sounds like the company is in great shape and has such great opportunities, so why are you selling?"* It's a seemingly innocent and logical question. In that moment, when you are putting a forkful of dessert in your mouth, you freeze. You know why you're selling, but you've never actually explained it to anyone out loud in a concise and meaningful way. The first thing that comes to mind is, *"I'm tired and need cash to retire."* What do you tell him?

This may actually be your reason for selling the business, but that's not how you should communicate your reason. Now the buyer is worried you're tired because the business isn't running as smoothly as you've indicated. If the business is so profitable, why would you want to sell it? Or, the buyer believes you're desperate to get out and views that as a negotiating tool for pricing. Either way, you've made a critical error and the sale process has just begun.

Where do I begin – why, who, what, when or how?

Begin with "why?"

Before you discuss selling your business with anyone, you must be able to articulate *why* you're selling your business to anyone who asks (potential buyers, employees, customers, suppliers, etc.). The message must be consistent with everyone. You can't say one thing to your management team and something different to a potential buyer or your customers. Be honest, but understand the words you choose have a significant impact on your message.

Rather than, "I'm tired and need cash to retire," a better explanation of *why* you are exiting might go like this: *"I've built a valuable business with great employees, and I believe there's a great future ahead for the business. It's simply time to create some liquidity for my family."*

Almost everyone will understand and generally accept this explanation. It reinforces the strength of the business and employees while providing a personal reason that doesn't get too personal. There might be several reasons why you need to create liquidity, but that doesn't need to be part of the discussion. Keep it crisp and simple.

> **Expert Insight:**
>
> **Be prepared to answer "what's next for you"**
>
> The most logical question will always be, "What's next for you?" or "What will you do after you exit your business?" This will be particularly important for potential buyers. If you have prepared yourself as we discuss in Part I, you should be able to answer this with confidence. If you aren't able to articulate what you're doing after the sale, the buyer might decide you're not ready to sell and won't spend the time and expense to go through the process with you. Remember, one of the primary reasons deals fail is that the seller is not prepared emotionally and financially to exit the business. Don't let poor communication with the potential buyer kill your deal.
>
> You cannot underestimate the importance of this point. There's a reason only one in four sell their business successfully.

Once you have the "why" down, you'll need to put together a detailed communication plan that addresses:

- <u>Who</u> you must communicate with
- <u>What</u> questions you will need to answer
- <u>When</u> you will communicate your plans
- <u>How</u> you will communicate your plans

Experienced advisors can be extremely helpful with creating your communication plan. Use their insight to make sure you are as prepared as possible.

Who must you communicate with?

There will be more interested parties than you realize asking you questions throughout the process. First, make a list of all parties you might need to communicate with, such as:

- Potential buyers
- Management
- Employees
- Customers
- Suppliers
- Other investors or shareholders (if applicable)
- Bank relationships
- General business community
- Friends and neighbors

Each of these parties will have different motivations behind their questions, which you'll need to think through when building your communication plan. Each party will want to know how the exit will impact them. It's critical your messaging is consistent between all parties while addressing their unique concerns.

- Potential buyers – What are your motivations for selling and do you have a plan for yourself after the sale?
- Management and employees – How will they be impacted personally? Will they still have jobs?
- Customers and suppliers – How will the sale impact their business relationship with the company going forward (pricing, product mix, etc.)?

- Bank relationships (lenders) – What will their relationship be with the new owner and will any outstanding debt be paid off at closing?
- Investors or other shareholders – What will the investors and shareholders receive upon the sale?
- Others – Why are you selling and how might the business change after the sale?

As you can see, there are several different ways to look at your communication plan. The next step in preparing a communication plan is to determine *what* you will communicate to all relevant parties.

What questions will you have to answer?

When thinking about the "what," it's again critical that your *message is always consistent to all parties*. Different parties hearing different messages causes fear, uncertainty and mistrust. This is usually unintentional on the seller's part. The seller simply hasn't prepared a comprehensive communication plan and practiced responses to questions.

We know a business owner, Scott, who told the buyer the reason he was exiting his business was to spend time with his family. During diligence, the buyer casually asked the management team why Scott was selling. Members of the team said it was because Scott was tired of the increasing regulatory environment in their industry and wanted to sell to a larger company who could afford the continuously increasing costs. Why would they say that to the buyer? That's what Scott had said to them during a moment of stress and exhaustion when he wasn't considering how his message would be taken. The buyer began wondering if he had underestimated the regulatory costs. As a result, the focus of diligence became the regulatory costs versus the growth opportunities of the business.

> **Expert Insight:**
>
> **Fill the communication void or it will be filled for you**
>
> In attempting to keep the transaction confidential, you may think it's better to say nothing than to try to address everyone's questions and concerns. Don't fall into this trap! Voids in communication will always be filled and generally not with the information you want. Be proactive and avoid having false information create a story that you can't overcome.

It's important to point out how a potential transaction might benefit the group you're addressing. Always address the "what's in it for me," or "WIIFM." For instance, customers may have access to a broader set of products than before or your employees might have more opportunities to advance within a larger company. Keep it positive and focused on them.

This is an enormous undertaking for you as the seller, both professionally and personally, and it's likely consuming your thoughts. Employees, customers and other parties will ask questions about you and your plans after the transaction. This is an exciting time for you, so it's tempting to tell them how the sale will benefit you and your finances, or about your exciting plans after you exit. It may seem like they want to hear all about you, but what they really want to know is how the transaction will impact them – the WIIFM. Move the conversation from you to them as quickly as possible. If you talk about how it benefits them, they might actually listen!

Online Resources: Tips for creating communication plans

> **Expert Insight:**
>
> ## Type of buyer can influence communication
>
> The type of buyer and the buyer's plans for the company post-sale will play a role in determining what you communicate to your management and employees.
>
> - Financial buyers – generally there is not a lot of change in the day-to-day operations of the company; the management team continues if the buyer has confidence in their abilities
> - Strategic buyers – if this buyer plans to integrate your business into theirs, there could be significant changes to the management team, employees and the processes and procedures in place at your business; requires more detailed communication throughout the process
> - Lifestyle buyers – similar to financial buyers, there is generally not a lot of change in the day-to-day operations of the business
>
> Consider who your potential buyer might be when determining what needs to be communicated to your management and employees.

When will you communicate?

The ultimate goal of the seller is to the keep the deal confidential for as long as possible. What if customers know about the deal, but it doesn't happen? What does that say about your business? Will customers assume the sale didn't happen because nobody wanted to buy your business? Is the logical conclusion the business is struggling? This is very tricky stuff, and we highly recommend you work with your advisors and the potential buyer to determine *when* to communicate with each set of parties.

The "when" is just as important as the "what" in your communication plan and should be coordinated with the potential buyer. Your communication plan should address typical questions you would receive from a variety of sources at each stage of your process (early stage, during the process, and at closing).

For example, here are some questions you might be answering from your management team at different stages:

- Early stage – Why are you selling?
- During the process – Who are you selling to? Will I have a job with the new owner? When will it happen?
- At closing – What will change in my job responsibilities? Who will I report to?

As we indicated above, you will likely need to get at least some of your management team involved early in the process to help you collect information for potential buyers. You won't know a lot of answers in the early stage, so keeping your management team updated regularly on the sale process will keep them engaged and focused.

Expert Insight:

Poor communication = loss of productivity

The Institute of Mergers, Acquisitions and Alliances estimates that during a transaction, at least two hours of productivity per day per employee are lost due to poor communication planning by the owner.

```
You                    Employees
┌──────────────┐    ┌──────────────┐    ┌──────────────┐
│     Poor     │───▶│  Uncertainty │───▶│     Fear     │
│ Communication│    │              │    │              │
└──────────────┘    └──────────────┘    └──────────────┘
                                               │
                                               ▼
                                        ┌──────────────┐
                                        │  Distraction │
                                        └──────────────┘
                                               │
                                               ▼
                                        ┌──────────────────┐
                                        │Loss of Productivity│
                                        │   and Quality    │
┌──────────────────┐                    └──────────────────┘
│ Profits Decline =│◀───────────────────────────┘
│Decrease in Price │
└──────────────────┘
```

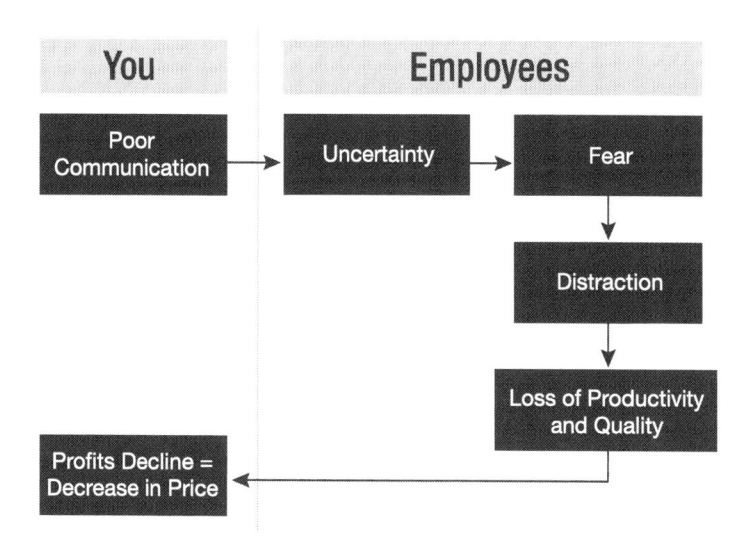

Loss of productivity during the sale process is a very real threat to a business. This is the worst time for productivity to decrease. You want your business to be as strong as possible during the sale process. Unfortunately, people talk and sometimes word of a potential sale gets around before a business owner is ready for employees to know. Don't ignore the rumors, as that will only exacerbate the distractions and potential loss in productivity.

The timing for communicating with customers and suppliers may not be completely within your control. You might want to wait until closing to disclose your plans, but the potential buyer might want to talk to your largest customers and most important suppliers as part of their diligence process. Discuss this with your advisors before allowing any discussions between the buyer and your customers or suppliers. You'll want to wait until you're as certain as possible the transaction is going to happen. This often becomes a sticky negotiating item with the buyer.

How will you communicate?

There are multiple ways to communicate, especially in this technology-driven world:

- In person
- In writing (memo, letter, press release)
- Via email
- On your website
- Social media

Each of these approaches has pros and cons depending on *what* information you're communicating to *who* and *when*. For example, if you're telling your management team for the first time about the transaction, you'll want to do that in person. Make sure you can answer their questions and read their body language throughout the discussion.

A general rule is that nothing should be in writing until you're prepared for broad distribution of the message. In today's world, even hard copy memos can be scanned and immediately sent to anyone, anywhere. To maintain confidentiality, try to do as much of your early communication in person as possible.

Most sellers and buyers prepare a list of frequently asked questions ("FAQs") to handle the most commonly asked questions of all interested parties. These FAQs are usually more general in nature and are available on your website or employee intranet. The FAQs should be developed in connection with the help of your advisors and your senior management team to ensure the messaging is appropriate and there are no legal issues with the information being distributed.

> **Expert Insight:**
>
> **Coordinate your communications with the buyer**
>
> You may feel confident you know how to communicate your plans and the exit process to everyone, but there will be certain questions you can't answer because the final decision will be up to the buyer. For example, "What employees will be retained by the new owner?" and "Will there be changes to employment arrangements?" are questions only the buyer can answer. The messaging and timing of when and what you communicate needs to be agreed upon by both you and the buyer.

Equip your team with the communication plan

Although we've talked a lot about how to communicate with your management and employees, *they* will also need to practice how to communicate with others about the transaction. For management, there is an additional requirement to communicate matters specific to their employees. This puts an extra stress on management, as they have to answer questions both internally and externally. Give your management team talking points to assist them in managing questions from employees and third parties.

How do your employees answer questions from customers about the transaction? Don't let them be caught off guard. Equip them with a communication plan to address questions they might receive from customers, suppliers or other outsiders to avoid inconsistent or misinformation in the market place.

Your team also includes your advisors. They could be asked questions by the buyer or other outside parties who have heard the rumor mill. Make sure your advisors are all on the same page regarding communication, especially with regard to the "when."

Practice, practice, practice...out loud

You've decided why, who, what, when and how to communicate with several different parties and have developed a communication plan that addresses potential questions each party might ask. You've shared that plan with your team. Now, you need to practice *out loud* delivering responses to the questions in the communication plan in a crisp, honest and consistent manner.

Why practice out loud? Remember the first time you spoke in front of a group? You'd rehearsed your speech dozens of times in your head and had it memorized to perfection. When you got up in front of the group and opened your mouth to speak, it didn't sound anything like what you'd practiced in your head. In fact, once you started hearing your voice, you forgot what you'd memorized.

> **Expert Insight:**
>
> **Amateurs practice until they get it right, professionals practice until they can't get it wrong.**
>
> Prepare your answers now to potential questions, review your answers with your advisors, then practice your responses out loud. You want your answers to be crisp, honest and consistent. Trust us, if you haven't practiced them out loud, they won't come out of your mouth as smoothly or professionally as you'd hoped.

Although it sounds odd and may prove uncomfortable for you, role-playing with your advisors is highly recommended. Anticipating the questions buyers might ask and rehearsing your answers with your advisors will make communication more natural for you and more effective overall.

> **Expert Insight:**
>
> **Every word you speak has consequences**
>
> Every word you speak and action you take throughout the process will be analyzed in detail by everyone impacted by the transaction. Be consistent and know the tone you want your message to have. It only takes one misstep in communication to create a loss of productivity in your employees, a loss of customers due to uncertainty, and a loss of a potential buyer due to lack of trust.

We began this chapter with three scenarios you may encounter during your exit process. We would love to give you the "right" solution to those scenarios, but we can't because there is no right answer. Each situation is unique. Your focus should be on understanding the types of questions you might get so you can develop a communication plan specific to *your* transaction.

17
Am I ready to move into the exit process?

So are you ready to move into the exit process? Before you answer, you should be able to state the following:

- I know what exit strategy is right for me.
- I have a clear financial plan in place.
- I know what I want to do with my life after the sale.
- I've estimated the value of my business.
- I've identified the value drivers and detractors of my business and put together a plan to address them.
- I've hired transaction advisors and developed a communication plan.

If you can make these statements, you're ready. It's time to move into the exit process.

PART II | Prepare Your Business **123**

Key takeaways from Part II – Prepare your business:

- Financial, Strategic and Lifestyle buyers have different traits and motivations you need to understand early in the process.
- There are three primary valuation approaches – market, asset and income (the most common).
- You should identify normalizing and pro forma adjustments to your financials prior to entering into an LOI.
- It's important to determine your walk-away price early in the process.
- Identifying the value drivers and detractors of your business is critical while preparing your business.
- Experienced advisors are critical to your success and you should select them wisely.
- The communication of your exit plans should be concise and consistent to all parties throughout the entire process.

Online resources referenced in Part II:

Buying this book gives you *free access* to online resources available through your Book Level Membership of **ExitBubble.com**, including, but not limited to, the resources referenced in *Part II*:

- Buyers' traits and motivations
- Pros and cons of valuation approaches
- Asset approach template
- Valuation analysis tool
- Normalizing and pro forma adjustments
- Value Profile worksheet
- Sample information request list
- Action plan template
- Advisors' roles and responsibilities
- Background checks on advisors
- Tips for creating communication plans

Go deeper in Exit Bubble Elite

Exit Bubble Elite provides you additional in-depth and personalized resources such as:

- Unlimited access to a comprehensive online valuation analysis tool with step-by-step video instructions.
- Interactive Value Profile tool included in the online valuation analysis tool that includes a detailed report to help you identify and prioritize your value drivers and detractors.
- Electronic copy of the book "*Ownership Thinking: How to End Entitlement and Create a Culture of Accountability, Purpose, and Profit*" (accompanied by videos) by best-selling author, Brad Hams, who shows you how to increase your company's productivity, employee retention, and profitability.
- Communication plan template with numerous example questions to prepare to answer at all stages of your exit process.

PART III

Exit Your Business

"...If I played well and prepared myself properly, then all I had to do was control myself and put myself in a position to win."

– *Jack Nicklaus*

18
Entering the exit process

In *Parts I* and *II*, you prepare yourself and your business for a potential exit. What if, after preparing yourself and your company, you decide <u>not</u> to exit your business in the near term? In that case, congratulate yourself on the hard work you've just completed and realize you are ahead of the game if and when you decide to exit your business in the future. Continue running your business with your exit in mind so you can exit when you're ready and/or when the market conditions are right.

If you decide to exit your business, read on. In *Part III*, we walk you through a transaction from structure to close, using the exit strategy of selling to a third party. Even if you've chosen an exit strategy of selling your business to your employees or transitioning it to the next generation, you will go through a process very similar to selling to a third party.

We've also made some assumptions about the order in which certain activities will occur. For example, we address management presentations in Phase II Diligence. Depending on your potential buyers and how you're running your sale process, you might give your management presentation during Phase I, then do it again to kick off Phase II for your buyer's advisors who did not hear the first presentation.

You might have multiple bidders and decide to enter into an LOI with two buyers instead of giving exclusivity to one buyer. Either way, you've still limited your negotiating power by limiting the number of potential buyers, and the steps you should take before entering into an LOI will still be applicable.

Every transaction is unique. Arm yourself with an understanding of the basic concepts, and you'll be able to successfully navigate any process.

Now that you've decided to exit, you're asking yourself a new set of questions:

- How long will it take to sell my business?
- What's the best transaction structure for me?
- How will I get paid?
- How do I attract buyers?
- How do I prepare for buyers' questions?
- How will I select the best buyer for my business?
- What will diligence look and feel like?
- What documents will I be signing?
- What happens on and after closing?

> **Expert Insight:**
>
> **Put yourself on a level playing field with buyers**
>
> This could be the first and only time you will sell a business. You'll typically be negotiating with experienced buyers. Some buyers look at hundreds, if not thousands, of deals, giving them a clear advantage over you. It's reasonable you're anxious about this new territory and don't want to feel you lack confidence or control. Knowing what's coming and what's in your control will help you effectively navigate the process, reduce your anxiety, and continue to perform at the top of your game.

Focus on what you can control in the process

As a business owner, you are experienced in managing relationships with employees, customers and suppliers, and are in control of most aspects of your professional life. In the sale process, there will be many factors you can't control. Additionally, you'll be dealing with a new set of constituents – advisors and buyers – all while continuing to run your business. This creates an emotional roller coaster that may feel overwhelming at times.

To reduce your anxiety and stress during this challenging process, we recommend you focus on what you *can* control (internal forces) and accept what you *can't* control (external forces).

What you can control:

- Your perceptions and emotions during the process
- The preparation of yourself and your company
- What, when and how you communicate the transaction
- The selection of your advisors
- The selection of your potential buyer

According to transaction advisors, one of the biggest mistakes sellers make is taking their eye off of day-to-day operations of their company. This is something else you *can* control. If you take your foot off the accelerator and company performance dips, buyers will start asking questions, diligence becomes more complicated, and your valuation could go down.

What you can't control:

- General markets
- The regulatory environment
- The economy

Specific to your sale process, you won't be able to control:

- The motivations of potential buyers
- The financing available for different types of buyers
- The buyer's valuation methodology and deal process

You can, however, influence the impact of some of these factors through preparation and communication, including the number of interested buyers, how your advisors work together, the duration of the sale process, and a buyer's perception of risk.

> **Expert Insight:**
>
> **What can you control?**
>
> When you find yourself overwhelmed with all the requirements of selling your business while also running it, identify the things you can control, accept the things you can't, and focus your energy appropriately.

How long will it take to sell my business?

Now that you've decided to sell your business and have hired advisors, you're ready to move quickly, right? Hold your horses. You want to take the time to do it right the first time so you don't have to do it – or earn it – again.

Many business owners we've talked to agree that it takes approximately six to twelve months to sell a business once you complete your preparations and *start* the sale process. The timeline varies based on a variety of factors: general economy; financing availability and interest rates; industry trends; size and complexity of the business; type and availability of buyers; and level of preparation of the seller, to name a few.

Example sale process timeline

Step	Action	Estimated Time to Complete
Structure/ Pitch Book	– Identify preferred deal structure – Prepare pitch book and teaser	30-60 days
Phase I Diligence	– Solicit interest from potential buyers – Prepare data room and management presentations	3-4 weeks minimum, up to 6-12 months 30-90 days
Letter of Intent (LOI)	– Buyer assessment – Execute a letter of intent	1-4 weeks
Phase II Diligence	– Detailed diligence – Address re-trade risk – Draft purchase documents	60-120 days
Closing	– Sign the documents – Celebrate! – What's next?	30 minutes The rest of your life….

The actual time it will take to complete each step will vary for each business depending on the factors described above. Keep in mind you're competing for the limited numbers of buyers in the Exit Bubble™. Knowing the process and what to expect will give you an advantage in navigating the shifting timeline and flatten the emotional roller coaster of the sale process. Be prepared. Be patient.

19

Structuring your transaction

Structure › Pitch Book › Phase I Diligence › LOI › Phase II Diligence › Close

What's the best transaction structure for me?

You've probably heard the horror stories of business owners closing on the sale of their businesses only to end up with overwhelming tax bills because the structure they chose had unintended tax consequences. For some, this meant they didn't have enough to retire and had to keep working. They had to earn it again.

To avoid this, you and your advisors need to determine the optimum transaction structure for you. Unfortunately, your buyer's optimum transaction structure is often different from yours because the buyer's motivations are different. Before you take your business to market, you'll need to understand how various transaction structures could impact your financial outcome at exit. Work closely with your advisors – tax attorney, CPA, and investment banker or broker, if applicable – to model the effect of the different structures so you are prepared in negotiations with a potential buyer.

> **Expert Insight:**
>
> **Don't jump without your tax advisor as your parachute!**
>
> What follows is meant to give you a basic understanding of the various deal structures: asset, stock and partial stock. We are not tax attorneys and don't know the specifics of your transaction. We are not providing legal or tax advice. It's critical that you consult your advisors on the complexities surrounding your specific transaction structure.

To begin, determine the best structure for you by asking yourself:

- When I sell my business, what am I actually selling—certain assets, my entire business, my brand?
- What type of company am I selling (e.g., **C-Corp**, **S-Corp**, **LLC**, **Partnership**, **Sole Proprietorship**)?
- What are the tax implications to me of each structure?

Defining the transaction structures

Asset sale

If the buyer purchases only specific assets, it is called an "asset sale." Under this structure, you may think you've sold the business, but you've really only sold part of it. You are still on the hook for the remaining liabilities of the company, both the known and potential **legacy liabilities** (e.g., litigation, facilities' leases, personal guarantees, tax liabilities, and contingent liabilities).

Legacy liabilities are liabilities related to the company prior to the sale that may or may not be known at the time of the sale.

As an example, you own Clean Company, a well-known manufacturer of "Clean Mops." You enter into an asset sale and sell all of your assets (facilities, inventory, receivables) and the brand name "Clean Mops" to a buyer. You still own the legal entity "Clean Company." After the sale, a customer sues Clean Company for defects in a mop they purchased before the sale. As the owner of Clean Company, you are responsible for the costs of defending the lawsuit.

> **Expert Insight:**
>
> **What liabilities are you responsible for?**
>
> As a seller, you need to be aware that, under an asset sale, you're still responsible for anything that occurred in the company prior to the asset sale (e.g., tax liabilities, environmental issues, product defect liabilities). This is true because your company still exists in its original legal form.

In preparing your business for sale, you should have identified your company's liabilities (known and potential). If you and the buyer choose an asset sale, you will be responsible for the remaining liabilities of the company until you're able to settle them and have dissolved the company.

In the *eyes of buyers*, this is the preferred structure because they choose the assets they want to purchase and leave you with the risk of known and unknown liabilities of the remaining legal entity. This may sound scary or unfair, but this may be the only option to get your deal done. If you need to sell your business quickly for personal reasons or you are struggling to find an ideal buyer, this might be a structure for you to consider.

Sole proprietors and single member LLCs

If you are a sole proprietor or a **single member LLC**, selling your business will always be considered an asset sale for tax purposes because the assets of your company are owned by you personally. For example, you might be the sole owner of an ice cream shop. All of the assets and liabilities of that shop (facilities, equipment, ice cream, and supplier payables) are owned by you personally versus a corporation or other entity. Selling the business would be considered selling your individual assets.

Stock sale

If you sell all of the shares of your company, it is called a "stock sale." This means you are selling everything. The buyer is now responsible for legacy liabilities. Sellers generally prefer this structure because they exit free and clear. Buyers will be concerned about unknown liabilities they might be inheriting. Because of this uncertainty, the buyer's diligence will generally be more extensive in a stock sale.

For example, if you sell products in several states, the buyer might spend a significant amount of time ensuring you have fully paid taxes in all of those states. A potential future tax liability could mean a discount in the buyer's purchase price. In an asset sale, this would not be a concern for the buyer as you would be responsible for those tax liabilities incurred prior to the sale.

Partial stock sale

This structure is often referred to as "taking some money off the table." Under this arrangement, you sell a majority of the stock of your company and retain a minority ownership interest (less than 50%). In a partial stock sale, you might agree to remain with the company in some capacity, in either an active role or a consulting role.

For instance, you own 100% of your business and decide to sell 80% of the business to a buyer and retain 20% for yourself. You monetize (get paid cash for) 80% of your business at closing. If the value of the business increases in the future, your 20% share will also increase in value *when the buyer sells to another party*. Stock in private, small businesses is typically not liquid. Unless and until the buyer sells the business to another buyer, there's likely limited or no ability to sell your 20% interest in the company. You might not be able to monetize the remaining 20% for a long time, if ever.

Some buyers want the seller to retain an interest in the business to accomplish two things:

- Allow the buyer to pay less "up front." The initial payment received by the seller is lower, but the potential future payout is significantly larger to the seller. This protects the buyer from over-paying up front.
- Provide continuity in the operations and customer relationships for the new owner after the sale.

Tax impacts of transaction structures

The tax impact of different transaction structures varies between the seller and buyer based on the corporate structure of the seller's business (C-Corp, S-Corp, **multi-member LLC**, **single member LLC**, Partnership or Sole Proprietorship) and can be extremely complex and transaction-specific. Different corporate structures have different tax results for sellers and buyers which are generally in direct conflict with each other, making negotiations tricky at times. The legal description of a transaction structure (asset or stock sale) is not necessarily how it is viewed for tax purposes. Not surprisingly, taxes are complicated!

> **Expert Insight:**
>
> ### Asset or stock sale?
>
> A seller should generally try to negotiate for a stock sale (or partial stock sale) versus an asset sale. An asset sale leaves the seller liable for legacy liabilities of the business. It also requires an allocation of the purchase price to your assets for tax purposes. Depending on how you and the buyer negotiate the allocation of the purchase price to the assets sold, your tax liability could vary significantly. Discuss your specific case with your advisors so that you understand the different tax impacts based on various allocation methods before agreeing to an asset sale.

Tax considerations of an asset sale

Sellers - The proceeds from an asset sale of entities other than C-Corps are generally taxed only once at the individual level based on the allocation of the purchase price to the assets sold. However, capital assets held more than a year will be taxed at capital gain rates and all other assets will be taxed at ordinary income rates. Also, some states impose a transfer tax on virtually all tangible personal property, such as vehicles, so consult your advisor for the rules in your state. Refer to the IRS definitions of different asset categories.

> Exception: Sellers of a C-Corp will generally be taxed at two levels in an asset sale:
> - Level 1 – at the corporate level on the sale of assets of the company. These proceeds will be taxed at the corporate tax rate of the company based on the excess of the sale price and tax basis of the assets.
> - Level 2 – at the individual level when proceeds from the sale of the assets are distributed to the owner(s). The owner would pay an additional layer of tax.

Buyers – In an asset purchase, buyers get a step-up in basis for the fair value of the assets they acquire. This allows them to have higher asset values to depreciate for tax purposes, which decreases their taxable income in the future. Legacy liabilities are generally not assumed by the buyer in an asset purchase, making this structure the preferred structure for most buyers.

Tax considerations of a stock sale

For purposes of our discussion, a stock sale also includes partial stock sales, sales of membership interests in multi-member LLCs, and sales of partnership interests in partnerships.

Sellers – Sellers generally have only one level of tax in a stock sale. You are taxed on the amount that the sale price of your stock exceeds your basis in the stock. For example, if you sell 100 shares of your company for $10 cash/share, and your tax basis in those shares is only $3/share, you would be taxed on $700 (the difference between $1,000 proceeds and $300 basis) at the capital gains rate. The seller is also not required to perform an allocation of the purchase price to assets sold.

Buyers - Buyers generally don't get a step-up in basis of the assets acquired in a stock purchase, so tax depreciation is not increased after the purchase. The buyer also generally assumes legacy liabilities of the company. This structure doesn't provide as many benefits to the buyer as an asset purchase.

> Exception: The purchase of multi-member LLCs and partnerships are generally treated for tax purposes as asset purchases for a buyer allowing for a step-up in basis of the assets and higher tax depreciation. This is one case where the tax treatment is different for the seller (stock sale) and buyer (asset purchase).

One thing to note. It may be possible for you to not be taxed (at closing) on any stock you receive as compensation instead of cash. If you are accepting stock for a portion or all of your consideration, consult your tax advisor on tax planning options.

Also remember the sale of single member LLCs and sole proprietorships should be treated as an asset sale for tax purposes for both the seller and buyer.

The discussion above is just the tip of the iceberg when it comes to taxes. We can't stress enough that you should consult your tax advisor on your specific transaction to understand the tax impact to you.

> **Expert Insight:**
>
> ### Minimizing "double taxation" for a C-Corp
>
> If you are a C-Corp, one way to minimize the double taxation at the corporate and shareholder level is to have the buyer pay a portion of the purchase price directly to you. This could be done by paying you for agreeing to a **non-compete agreement**, entering into a consulting agreement, or paying you a reasonable bonus when the transaction closes. You might also get the buyer to pay you for some intangible value that you've personally built in the business, such as long-standing customer or supplier relationships. This "personal goodwill" is difficult to quantify, but could be an option for minimizing the taxes at the corporate level if your buyer is willing to consider this approach. Make sure your tax advisor helps you consider the tax impact of the above options to both the buyer and seller.

How and when will I get paid for my business or assets?

Now that you've established the structure that works best for you and understand the tax implications of that structure, you need to determine how and when you want to get paid for your business:

- Do you want to receive all cash or a combination of cash and the buyer's stock?
- Do you want to receive one payment up front or a portion of the payment deferred in an "earn-out" or by providing seller financing?

Receiving cash versus the buyer's stock

Depending on your financial needs after you exit, you will want to determine what form of payment you want from the buyer. Most owners prefer actual dollars when they sell their business so they can cash out and move on to their next adventure. However, the buyer may have limited cash resources or simply choose to pay a certain amount in cash and give the seller shares of the buyer's stock for the remainder of the purchase price.

Taking the buyer's stock minimizes the amount of cash the buyer has to pay and potentially minimizes the amount of taxes due by the seller. It also puts an extra burden of risk on the seller. As discussed in the partial stock sale description above, the stock of a private, small business is not liquid. There's always a risk you will not be able to sell it in the future.

Consider these questions when taking stock as part of your consideration:

- Am I willing and able to take less cash up front?
- Am I willing to take on the risk of the buyer's stock value declining in the future?
- Will I be able to sell my stock in the future?

If you decide to take stock, you'll need to perform diligence on the buyer to make sure you agree with the value assigned to the buyer's stock at closing and to understand the potential for that stock value to decline in the future.

For example, you take the buyer's stock that is valued at $10/share at the time of the sale. The new owner decides to modify your product to lower the cost, but in doing so loses a significant customer due to quality issues. The value of your stock may now be $5/share. You've effectively lost half of your proceeds from the stock portion of your sale price. Before you decided to take stock in the new company, did you ask about the new owner's plans for the products? Did you know there were material changes to the business planned after the sale?

> **Expert Insight:**
>
> ### Do your own diligence
>
> It's important to do your diligence on a buyer in general, but especially if you're taking stock and becoming an investor in the company after the sale. Ask questions similar to what they will be asking you. We discuss diligence in Chapter 23.

Earn-outs – a good strategy?

An earn-out is a negotiation strategy typically used to close perceived pricing gaps between seller and buyer. For example, a seller wants $10 million for a business. A buyer may offer to pay $8 million in total proceeds at closing. Alternatively, the buyer might offer $6 million at closing and an additional $4 million over a three- to five-year period based on the company achieving specified milestones. The result is that the *potential total* purchase price ($10 million) in an earn-out structure will be greater than what the seller receives in one up-front payment ($8 million).

An earn-out can look appealing to a seller because of the larger total possible purchase price. In practice, an earn-out is one of the most common causes of legal disputes between sellers and buyers.

Buyers use an earn-out to minimize the risk of overpaying for the company up front (i.e., paying now for results that may not happen in the future). They want to pay the additional purchase price only if the company actually performs in the future in terms of negotiated targets. Sellers might want an earn-out if they are confident the performance criteria will be met, and they can afford to look at the future payment as a bonus (i.e., the up-front payment is sufficient for their exit needs).

The most common targets used in earn-outs are financial targets (revenues, net income, EBITDA), but you might see other targets such as customer retention, operating metrics, or product development milestones depending on the type of company. An earn-out can be structured as annual payments of fixed dollar amounts or as a percentage of a financial measure with a cap on the total dollar amount. Generally, the earn-out term is no longer than three years. The longer the term, the more likely significant changes could occur that reduce the company's ability to meet the targets and increase the risk of the seller not getting paid in full.

> **Expert Insight:**
>
> ### How confident are you in your projections?
>
> As a seller, you will likely tell the buyer you are highly confident in your company's ability to meet the projections you provided during diligence. In an earn-out, the buyer will likely use those projections to set the earn-out targets. Make sure they're realistic and attainable or you could find yourself in a very awkward situation when negotiations for an earn-out begin. The buyer will wonder why they should rely on the projections if you're not willing to base a portion of your proceeds on achieving them.

Although it's not always the case, an earn-out often involves the owner staying involved in the company in some fashion through the earn-out period (CEO, president, or consulting role). Staying involved, however, does not mean you have control. Remember, you no longer own the business. This can be very frustrating and can result in future disagreements between you and the new owner. The need to consider the challenges of transitioning to a new role is discussed in *Part I*.

Sellers must accept that, because they are no longer in control of the business, they may have little or no ability to influence the achievement of the specified milestones of the earn-out. Take, for instance, a case where you sold your distribution business and agreed to an earn-out of an additional $250,000 that would be paid if profits reached $500,000 in year one and $1,000,000 in year two. During year one, the owner decides to increase salaries and invest in a new product line. Expenses are much higher than forecasted, the profits don't meet the earn-out targets you agreed to—and you don't get paid the $250,000. Unfortunately, since you're not the owner, you are not able to control what happens in the company during that time. The new owner decided to make investments for the long term and it impacted the payment of your earn-out over the short term.

Make sure you have looked at the positives and negatives of entering into an earn-out arrangement before you make the decision.

Positives of an earn-out:

- Could provide significantly higher total proceeds received by the seller (up-front payment plus future payment)
- Could be a negotiating tool to getting a deal done more quickly when valuation prices are far apart
- May be the only way to get a deal done in a competitive market for buyers

Negatives of an earn-out:

- The risk of the transaction working as agreed transfers to the seller (i.e., buyer only pays if the future results are achieved)
- The deferred payment may never be earned and paid to the seller, thus it should be viewed as a bonus to the seller
- The seller may not have enough control over the future results of the company to ensure the earn-out gets paid
- It may be difficult to measure the results if your company is integrated into the buyer's operations
- The new owner may not provide additional capital to achieve growth goals anticipated in the earn-out targets

> **Expert Insight:**
>
> **Don't overlook the tax impact of earn-outs**
>
> The most common mistake we see sellers make in an earn-out is not understanding how the earn-out structure will impact the seller's tax treatment. In general, putting caps on earn-out payments and establishing shorter terms for the payout period cause fewer tax problems. This is a very complex area and should be discussed with your tax advisor based on your specific transaction.

Online Resources: Tips for negotiating earn-outs

Seller financing

Another option that helps small, private business owners sell their businesses is to offer seller financing to the buyer. Like earn-outs, this is a method of closing the pricing gap between seller and buyer. In this option, the seller provides the buyer with a loan at an agreed interest rate for a portion of the purchase price. This option is most common in smaller transactions with lifestyle buyers or a small company that doesn't have the ability to pay the entire purchase price up front. This is also often used for family and employee buyouts. Of course, like any loan, there is always a risk the borrower (buyer) will not be able to pay.

Unlike earn-outs, the future payments are based on a set schedule and are not dependent on meeting specific performance conditions. The buyer will likely use cash generated by the business in the future to make the loan payments, so if the company doesn't perform, there is a risk the buyer won't be able to repay the loan.

Given the risk of not being repaid, why would sellers choose to finance the sale of their business? Depending on the size of your business, the type of buyers who are interested in your business, and your immediate cash needs, this may be the only option that allows you to sell your business on your desired timetable. One way to help mitigate the risk of this option is for the buyer to guarantee the payments (personally and through the buyer's business). Accepting a buyer's guarantee isn't enough, though. You'll need to perform your own diligence on the buyer's financial health, including any assets that can be pledged as collateral on the loan. You can't completely erase the risk of repayment, but you can certainly be proactive in ensuring you have some protection.

You should also ensure in the terms of the financing document that you have access to the financial records of the business after the sale. Make sure you can monitor the performance and cash flows of the business and the likelihood of your loan being repaid.

Like an earn-out, seller financing only works if you are willing to delay the receipt of cash from the sale. Will you still be able to achieve your exit goals? Are you willing to delay some of those plans while waiting for the additional cash?

Do I want or need a role in the new company?

If you want to sell your business, receive all of your proceeds up front, and have no continuing ties to your business, this question probably isn't critical to you. If you have deferred a portion of your proceeds and the payment of those proceeds depends on the company's future performance, you may want or be required to remain with the company for a period of time. If you stay, how will you feel being part of the company but not the owner? Will you be okay with not being the final decision-maker?

We generally see sellers take on one of three roles: remain CEO, become president or head of sales, or become a consultant. The first two roles involve your active involvement in the company, which may not work for you personally, but may be the best opportunity for you to impact the results of the company in the future. As a consultant, a seller's role is on an as-needed basis as opposed to day-to-day.

Whatever your role will be, it's essential that you *clearly* define your responsibilities *prior* to closing the sale.

20
Finding a buyer

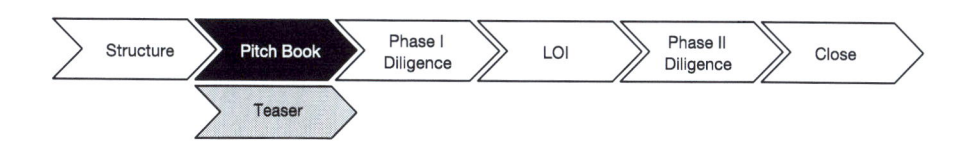

Structure › **Pitch Book** › Phase I Diligence › LOI › Phase II Diligence › Close

Teaser

How do I attract buyers?

Now that you've determined the structure that works best for you, it's time for you to market your business and attract potential buyers. This is primarily accomplished through a pitch book (also referred to as a confidential information memorandum or "CIM"). A pitch book tells the story of your business in enough detail to entice the buyer to want to enter into a letter of intent so they can dig deeper. It's a critical document in the sale process, as potential buyers will base their initial offers on the information included in the pitch book.

Think of a pitch book as the sales brochure of your business. When you sell a home, your realtor creates a brochure that lists the basic specifications (bedrooms, bathrooms, square feet) and also details the unique aspects of the home (home theater system, top-of-the-line appliances, walk-in closets). What will your sales brochure say about your business? Will buyers find your business attractive based on the information presented in the pitch book?

What goes in a pitch book?

The pitch book covers all aspects of your business, from the history of the operations to the forecasts and everything in between. In it, you'll discuss how your business began, historical financial results, and the strengths of your current management team. You might also describe your unique position in the market place, why your product is different from your competitors, and other differentiating factors.

There are many forms of pitch books. They can be formal or informal documents depending on the type of business you're selling and the type of buyers you're trying to attract. Regardless of the type of pitch book you choose to prepare, you should consider addressing the areas below in your communication with potential buyers:

1. Executive summary
   - Description of your business, including corporate strategy
   - Key investment considerations for a buyer
   - Summary financials
   - Proposed transaction structure
2. Industry overview
3. Company overview
   - History of your business
   - Marketing and sales organization
   - Operations
   - Major customers and suppliers
4. Competitive landscape
   - Summary of competition and your market position
5. Management
   - Organizational chart and management bios

6. Financial information
   - Historical financial statements for the past three years
   - Adjustments to historical financials for non-recurring or personal expenses
   - Forecasts for the next three years
7. Summary and next steps
   - Other information that would be relevant to buyers (differentiating factors)
   - Your timetable for the transaction

If you own a small business, this list may look daunting and not relevant to you. Keep in mind the information will be relevant to buyers of any size company, though the pitch book itself may be shorter than for a larger or more complex business. The key to an effective pitch book is to make the reader want to know more. A good pitch book will help draw interest from several buyers.

Online Resources: Top 10 tips for pitch books

How is a pitch book prepared?

After all the time you've spent preparing your business for sale, you're thinking the pitch book will take no time at all. Don't count on it. It must not only communicate facts, but also present your business (the good and the bad) in the most positive way possible. You only get one shot at a first impression, so take the time to get it right.

The process for preparing a pitch book can take 30-60 days or longer (depending on the complexity of your business) and is typically as follows:

1. Transaction advisor interviews the seller to get an in-depth understanding of the business, including the value drivers and detractors (discussed in *Part II*).
2. Transaction advisor provides the seller with a request list detailing the information needed to complete the pitch book.
3. Transaction advisor performs extensive research on your industry and market.
4. Seller gathers data/information requested by transaction advisor.
5. Transaction advisor writes the pitch book.
6. Seller reviews and verifies accuracy of data and message.

If you are not using a transaction advisor, you will be responsible for gathering the data and writing your pitch book. Regardless of who is writing the pitch book, don't underestimate the time it will take you to complete this task. We recommend you enlist other advisors or members of your management team to help compile the data and review the final document.

Why does it take so much time to prepare a pitch book? A good transaction advisor will spend time doing extensive research on your business, including your market and industry. A deep understanding of your business allows your transaction advisor to prepare an effective pitch book and be prepared to answer questions from potential buyers during the early stages of the marketing process. Take the time to educate your transaction advisor so he or she can effectively market your business and directly answer buyers' initial questions, allowing you to focus on running the business.

If you prepared your business as discussed in *Part II*, you likely developed a robust process for tracking key performance indicators. You should have a good understanding of the underlying trends and risks of your business as seen through the *eyes of the buyer*. That preparation will be helpful in the pitch book process, but you will need to go deeper. Gathering detailed information and framing it appropriately in the pitch book can be very time consuming. How do you juggle these demands with those of running your business?

Two considerations will help you navigate this challenge:

1. Having an understanding of the entire process before you get started should help you better manage the time requirements of the sale process. Keep in mind this is a marathon, not a sprint. If you pace yourself and plan accordingly, you can better handle the added burden of this second job.
2. Consider whether you want to get more of your management team involved to lessen the burden on your time. There is a risk that getting management involved will take too much focus away from the business. However, if you get the right people involved at the right time, this can be a lifesaver. They can help review the pitch book for accuracy, provide input into additional differentiators of your business, and help with framing the overall story of the business.

When and how to involve additional members of your management team will depend on the type of relationship you have with them, how much help you need and the importance of confidentiality to you. We discuss communicating with your management team in more detail in *Part II*.

> ### Gut Check: Ready for your "second job?"
> Until now, everything you've done to prepare for the sale has kept you focused on the business in some manner (working in it and on it). The sale process creates a whole new job for you that will take your time and focus away from your business. Don't jump into the process until you are really prepared!

It's your story – own it!

Your transaction advisor may actually compile and write the pitch book, but *you* are still responsible for the information that goes into it. It must be accurate and fairly represent your business, including any weaknesses you've identified during your preparation. You should review all information that is presented and make sure you can support it when speaking with potential buyers. This is your reputation on the line.

Why is it as important to talk about potential weaknesses or issues as it is to highlight the great aspects of your business? Buyers use this information to make their initial offer. The information in the pitch book becomes the basis for all discussions going forward. While it seems counter-intuitive to highlight any negatives, you don't want the buyer to be surprised after you've signed a letter of intent. The buyer will likely find it even if you don't disclose it. With surprises, the buyer will question your integrity and wonder what other issues you haven't disclosed. Surprises provide an opportunity for the buyer to negotiate the purchase price down, and after the LOI, you have less negotiating leverage.

As we discuss in *Part II*, different types of buyers will react differently to issues or weaknesses within your business depending on their objectives in purchasing your company.

For example, you may know your suppliers are planning to increase their prices in 90 days, but you don't disclose this information in the pitch book. You sign an LOI with a financial buyer who has a slightly higher initial offer price than a strategic buyer who was also interested in your business.

The financial buyer begins diligence, and the increased supplier pricing is discovered causing projected profits to decline. The financial buyer now wants to reduce the agreed-upon price in the LOI to less than what the strategic buyer originally offered due to reduced future profits. The financial buyer now begins to question the validity of everything you've disclosed.

The strategic buyer planned to use its own suppliers after the sale and was not concerned about your supplier's pricing increases. If you had disclosed this information while you still had the strategic buyer in the bidding process, you might have chosen to sign a LOI with the strategic buyer and achieved a higher purchase price.

> **Expert Insight:**
>
> **Minimizing re-trade risk**
>
> When a buyer negotiates a reduction in the purchase price after signing a letter of intent, this is called a "re-trade." You've already eliminated other potential buyers, so you have limited negotiating power. To minimize re-trade risk, disclose all of your issues prior to the letter of intent while you still have interest from multiple buyers.

While it's important to disclose issues, you should also talk about mitigating factors or why those issues shouldn't be material to the value of your business. Frame your issues in the most positive way possible while remaining factual.

For example, last year you lost your biggest customer and the sales numbers dropped. Explain why you lost the customer. Did your competitor "buy" your customer by cutting the margins by 50%? Did your sales team make a mistake? Maybe you identified that the products they were buying weren't profitable to you, and you gave your biggest (and worst) customer to one of your competitors. What actions did you take to replace that revenue, market share and profit? Did you hire additional sales reps, re-engineer your products, or reduce costs through operational efficiencies?

Every company has challenges and weaknesses. Proactively disclosing issues and showing that you have a plan to address them will make the buyer more comfortable with your overall story.

> **Expert Insight:**
>
> ### Be able to support your pitch book
> During diligence with the buyer you choose to move forward with, you must be able to support whatever information goes into the pitch book. Make sure you have reviewed all of it and can support every statement. Your credibility is on the line. Don't blow it.

Teaser

Once the pitch book is completed, your transaction advisor (or you) might prepare a one- to two-page summary of the pitch book called a teaser. The teaser would be sent to a broad group of potential buyers to determine initial indications of interest. The teaser generally doesn't give the name of your company and should be carefully written to protect your confidential information. If buyers are interested in learning more, they will sign a **non-disclosure agreement** (**NDA**) so they can receive the pitch book.

> **Expert Insight:**
>
> **NDAs are critical to the process**
>
> It's critical that you receive an NDA prior to providing any information to a third party. It's often tempting to send information to a friend or business acquaintance without asking for an NDA because you feel uncomfortable asking for one. Or, you might feel like it's not really sensitive information. Don't fall into that trap. You don't want that friend or business acquaintance to unknowingly or accidently share your company's information with a potential buyer or a competitor. Don't underestimate the value of your company's information to a potential competitor. It's better to be safe than sorry!

For smaller companies, a seller may decide that a teaser is all that is needed to distribute to potential buyers. Don't assume because your company is small the potential buyer will not eventually want all of the details you would normally include in a pitch book. Be prepared for more detailed questions from the potential buyer regardless of the size your company.

> **Gut Check: Are you ready?**
>
> Once you've hired advisors and have begun to circulate your teaser, it is very possible word will get out among your customers, competitors, suppliers or employees. How will you answer questions at this stage? As we discuss in Part II, you should have a detailed communication plan prepared with practiced responses to different parties at each stage of the transaction. Before you send out the teaser and pitch book, review your communication plan to prepare for possible questions.

21
Phase I Diligence – the dance begins

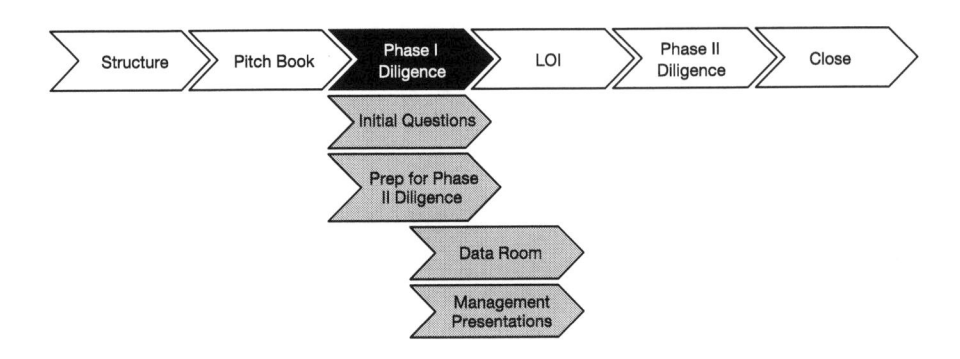

```
Structure  >  Pitch Book  >  **Phase I Diligence**  >  LOI  >  Phase II Diligence  >  Close
                                  │
                                  ├─> Initial Questions
                                  ├─> Prep for Phase II Diligence
                                  ├─> Data Room
                                  └─> Management Presentations
```

The teaser has been sent out. The pitch book is ready for potential buyers who sign an NDA and want more information on your business. What's next for you and your management team? Can you get back to running your business full-time while waiting for the ideal buyer to give you an offer? The reality is no. The sale process is just beginning. You will now move into Phase I Diligence, where you answer initial questions from potential buyers and prepare for Phase II Diligence. A strong management team will be critical to keep your business running during the sale process.

Initial questions from potential buyers

During Phase I Diligence, you will answer initial questions from potential buyers who are determining their level of interest in your company. Generally, these questions are a bit more detailed than your transaction advisor can answer, but not as detailed as Phase II Diligence, which generally occurs once a letter of intent has been signed.

> **Expert Insight:**
>
> **Questions intensify**
>
> More questions? You've already answered so many questions while preparing your pitch book; how could there possibly be more? Get ready, because now the number and nature of questions will increase and intensify as multiple buyers look for more information and move through the sale process. This is where differences between types of buyers become important (see detailed buyer discussion in Part II). You need to prepare yourself for the varied perspectives and motivations of multiple potential buyers.

Although there are multiple perspectives you may have to address, the starting point for information and data is typically the same for all buyers. The **information request list** (also called a data request list or diligence checklist) is a list of all the documents potential buyers will want to review *before* they begin to ask more detailed questions. We also discuss this list in *Part II*. This list will seem comprehensive to you, but remember, the checklist is the *minimum* amount of data the buyer will request. Hopefully, through preparing your business and the process of compiling information for the pitch book, you've gathered a lot of this data already.

Online Resources: Sample information request list

Preparing for Phase II Diligence

There are two primary activities you and your management team will focus on during Phase I Diligence to prepare for Phase II Diligence (other than, of course, running the business).

1. Data Room - creating a centralized location for data to be shared with the potential buyer
2. Management Presentations – preparing presentations your management team will give to the prospective buyer

Data room – the details behind your story

The data from the IRL will be maintained in a "data room," a fancy term for a centralized location for your company's data that can be accessed by potential buyers. There are two types of data rooms, physical and virtual. Before the Internet, a data room was, literally, a room filled with boxes of data pertaining to the seller's company (financial, legal, operations, employees, etc.). Now, most data rooms are maintained on a secure website only the seller and potential buyer can access. Over the years, the cost of a virtual data room has become attractive for almost any size transaction. There are a variety of virtual data rooms to choose from with various pricing options.

The benefits of a virtual data room include:

- The data is offsite from your location, away from employees and other stakeholders, making it easier to maintain confidentiality.
- There is less disruption to your management team because buyers review the data offsite, rather than on your premises.
- Buyers generally favor virtual data rooms which allow them to review information on their own timetable and eliminate the costs of traveling to review boxes of documents at your location.

Despite the benefits of a virtual data room, physical data rooms are still a viable option for some. Sellers who don't mind having potential buyers in their offices, or don't want to spend money for a virtual data room or time scanning all of their documents onto a website, may prefer the traditional room of boxes.

Discuss the pros and cons of both types of data rooms with your advisors to understand what they believe the potential buyers of your company will want – and consider what will best fit your needs as well.

> **Online Resources: Comparison of virtual and physical data rooms**

Does a data room apply to you?

You may be a small proprietorship wondering, "How does a data room relate to me?" Wouldn't it be more appropriate to apprentice the buyer in your business before you close the deal? Possibly, but you still need to provide a data room equivalent. Here's why:

In treating your buyer as an apprentice for a period of time before closing, you're providing an education on your customers, suppliers, facilities, pricing, leases, taxes and general business issues you face on a daily basis. You may not need a data room in the form we discuss above, but your apprentice will still need to know the information normally included in the data room before taking over the business from you.

Instead of creating an actual data room, you and, down the line, the next owner, will benefit if you take time to go through the IRL to make sure you're addressing all of the critical areas of your business.

> **Expert Insight:**
>
> **Get it out of your head**
>
> You know everything about your business – customer terms, selling and service agreements, supplier agreements, inventory levels, product specifications, business processes – much of which may not be documented anywhere. Although it may seem like a lot of the IRL may not apply to you, it's still a valuable exercise to ensure you've covered everything, including the vital pieces of information that may only be found in your brain.

Organizing your data room

Appearance counts

Before we discuss the inner workings of a data room, you should know the golden rule that applies: **Appearances are (almost) everything.** Data rooms must be organized and complete. Think about selling a house. After you've made improvements and before you start showing it, you need to put the final touches on it. Clean closets and organized kitchen cabinets tell the buyer you've taken good care of the house and reduce concerns there are hidden issues. The same applies for a data room.

A well-organized and complete data room goes a long way in building trust with a potential buyer. Even if the data doesn't tell a great story, the buyer gets a good feeling about the accuracy of the information and has an overall better feeling about how you run your company.

A data room is generally organized into four major areas:

1. *Legal/Corporate* – typically the largest section, which includes all legal documents and contracts related to the business (employee, customer, lease, etc.).
2. *Employees and Human Resources* – includes details on employees, compensation, benefit plans, employment agreements.
3. *Operational* – includes overviews of processes associated with running the business, including business relationships with suppliers and customers.
4. *Financial* – includes up to three years of historical information, details of specific balance sheet and income statement accounts, and your financial forecasts. This is also where you will show your normalized financials that exclude personal expenses and other non-recurring items. (Normalized financial statements are discussed in *Part II*.)

How should a data room be organized?

Your data room should be organized and indexed to match the numbering on either your version of the IRL or the potential buyer's IRL. If possible, designate one person to review all of the information placed into the data room. No matter how prepared and organized you think you are, with the large number of documents going into the data room, there's always the possibility you'll include incorrect or inconsistent information. This could prove disastrous during diligence, as we've seen.

One seller we know, John, put two separate copies of a balance sheet in the data room, both with an "as of September 30th" date. The balance sheets were indexed to different areas of the data room, and he assumed they were the same. As it turned out, one was a draft and the other was a final version of the balance sheet (including all accruals) – seemingly a simple error which could be easily explained. However, John was caught off guard and could not explain the differences between the two balance sheets during diligence.

The buyer became concerned and began to question the accuracy of all the information in the data room. The diligence process became much more detailed (and painful for John!). The buyer found other minor inconsistencies in the data room and was never quite comfortable with the quality of the information. The buyer pulled out of the deal – and it all started because of a simple error that could have been avoided.

Your designated reviewer should check for consistency among and between the documents placed in the data room and for accuracy in general. Think of it as a mini-audit of your information.

Protect sensitive information

While consistency and accuracy are critical, you must also decide if there is confidential and sensitive information you don't want to disclose early in the process. You may be concerned a potential strategic buyer will use customer pricing information to compete with you for that customer if they decide *not* to buy your company. Personal and sensitive information about your employees should never be posted in a data room where there is a risk of information leaking.

Protecting your confidential information is important, and you should discuss how to handle it with your advisors.

Online Resources: Tips for protecting sensitive information

Don't underestimate the time commitment of creating a data room

As with the pitch book process, don't underestimate the time it takes to compile information for your data room. Most of us don't make a habit of organizing our administrative/legal documents well (i.e., documents that aren't required to run the business on a day-to-day basis), or we keep them offsite at our attorney's office. Start identifying the location of these documents and organizing them now.

> **Expert Insight:**
>
> **It's never too early to start populating your data room**
>
> If you believe in "begin with the end in mind," then you should always be populating your data room in preparation for a potential exit. As you come across documents you think might be relevant to a potential buyer, especially legal documents, gather them in one place (either physically or virtually). This will not only put you ahead of the game when it's time to create your official data room, but will keep you in the mindset of preparing your business for exit.

The data room should be complete and ready for the buyer to access when the LOI is signed and the clock starts ticking on Phase II Diligence. You may want to give access to certain, high level information in the data room before the LOI is signed to help potential buyers develop a more informed initial offer.

Management presentations

Data is important, but it's only data until you pull it all together into a cohesive story and present it to the potential buyer. Your buyers don't understand the nuances of your business; they need you and your team to explain the story behind the data.

Just like the data room, appearances are (almost) everything in management presentations. If you appear confident, are able to articulate the strengths and challenges of your business, and are prepared to answer questions, you'll give your potential buyer a high level of comfort. If the buyer is comfortable from the start, Phase II Diligence will be less painful for everyone, especially you!

Depending on the number and type of prospective buyers, you may choose to deliver your presentation during Phase I Diligence or wait until the LOI is signed. Your transaction advisor can help you navigate the timing of these presentations.

Why make a formal presentation?

Management presentations accomplish two things:

1. Allow you to add details and color to the information in the pitch book. You can never get everything you want to tell a buyer in the pitch book. Verbally, you're able to expand on the strengths of your business and proactively address any weaknesses in more detail and in your own words.
2. Allow your management team to shine. When key members of your management team tell the story with you, it shows the strength of your team and initiates relationships with the buyer. Putting faces to

the names on an organizational chart can make that crucial difference as you move through the diligence process.

> **Gut Check: Don't get caught unprepared**
>
> Your management presentation could be the first time the buyer has a chance to ask questions of you directly. You and your team must begin preparing and practicing your presentation well in advance of presenting to a potential buyer. Adhere to the golden rule: "Amateurs practice until they get it right, professionals practice until they can't get it wrong."

You'll want to practice both the rehearsed part of the presentation and answering possible questions the buyer and buyer's advisors might ask you. Engage your advisors with this critical step.

- Ask your advisors to listen to your presentation with an objective view to help identify where there are inconsistencies or where the buyer might naturally ask questions.
- Have your advisors ask you questions the buyer might ask and practice *who* on your team will answer them and *how*.
- When answering a question, try to reference a page in your presentation or pitch book to provide depth and credibility to your answer.

Inconsistencies between the pitch book, the data room and the management presentation will lead to increasingly deeper questions from the buyer. They will call into question the accuracy of the data, the quality of your management team or, in the worst case, your integrity. Make sure you have completed your mini-audit and reviewed all information for accuracy and consistency. Then relax – you'll be as prepared as you can be.

Who should make the presentation?

Who from management should participate in the presentations? The answer to that question depends on a variety of factors. Ask yourself the following questions:

- If I were buying my company, who would I want to talk to?
- Who has been involved in creating and executing the overall strategy of the business?
- Who is responsible for running the business on a day-to-day basis?
- Who would be expected to continue with the company under the new owner?
- Who from my team has been told about the potential transaction?
- Is confidentiality with my management team still a concern?

Depending on the size of your management team and how you answer the questions above, you might decide you can handle the presentation by yourself. Make sure you're considering the type of questions that may come up and whether you will be able to answer them in sufficient detail.

At a minimum, there should always be someone who can speak in detail about the financials. You might be able to do that, but this is the area where inconsistencies in data and information really become critical. Will you be able to answer their detailed financial questions during that initial presentation? The presentation sets up the rest of Phase II Diligence. You want it to go smoothly and for the buyer to have positive perceptions throughout the process. You may be an inexperienced seller. Be prepared so you can level the playing field with a potentially more experienced buyer.

> **Expert Insight:**
>
> ### It's a marathon, not a sprint
>
> You are now working two full-time jobs, running your business and selling your business. Preparation is critical. Knowing what to expect will help you spread the work and distractions over a longer period to minimize the impact to your business. Think of this process as a marathon, not a sprint. If you can pace yourself over a longer period of time, the pain of the race will not be as severe!

22

Negotiating the letter of intent

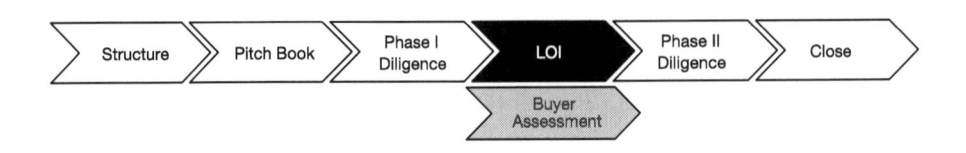

The letter of intent – the point of (almost) no return

Once you have a sufficient level of interest from buyers (hopefully more than one!), you or your advisors will ask them to provide initial offers. You'll review those initial offers with your advisors and determine which buyer you want to ask to put their terms into an offer letter, or letter of intent (LOI).

The LOI typically narrows the field to just one buyer to move with into Phase II Diligence. You are now in an exclusive arrangement with that buyer. Select your buyer and negotiate your LOI thoughtfully. Once you've entered into exclusivity, you've lost your ability to negotiate with multiple buyers.

If you're lucky enough to have multiple offers and decide to enter into LOIs with two or three buyers, that helps your negotiating power as you move through Phase II Diligence.

> **Expert Insight:**
>
> **The LOI price is not final**
>
> Except for the exclusivity and confidentiality clauses, the LOI is generally a non-binding offer to purchase your company and is subject to Phase II Diligence. This is a key point. Most sellers assume the price they negotiate in the LOI will be the final price for the transaction. This is not always the case. Phase II Diligence is just like a home inspection. You enter into a contract subject to an inspection by the buyer. If the inspection comes back with a plumbing problem, the buyer may want a discount on the price to compensate for the cost and effort of fixing the plumbing issue. There's always a risk that the buyer will find something that will be used to support a discount to the LOI price (known as a re-trade risk).

The LOI typically addresses, at a minimum, the following factors:

- Price and method of valuation (for example, a multiple of EBITDA or book value).
- Structure of the transaction. Will they pay in cash or stock? How will they finance their acquisition? Do they want to buy your entire company (stock purchase) or just certain assets and liabilities (asset purchase)?
- Exclusivity. Generally there is an agreement you will not "shop" your company to other buyers for a specified period of time (generally 30-60 days) while the buyer completes diligence.
- Expected timing to close. An exclusivity clause generally requires a purchase agreement be drafted by a certain date, which means you will need to understand when the buyer will be able to close. How long it

takes for buyers to get approval and how they will fund the transaction are generally the biggest factors impacting timing.
- Termination (break-up) fee. Sometimes there are break-up fees negotiated to ensure the buyer and seller are serious about completing a transaction. More often than not, the fee equates to the transaction/advisor costs incurred through the termination date by the other party.

How will the purchase price be determined?

In *Part II*, we discuss valuation methods the buyer might use to value your business and potential adjustments to the purchase price that might be negotiated during diligence. Now, let's discuss how the purchase price might be described and calculated in the **purchase and sale agreement** (**PSA**).

There are several different ways of determining the ultimate purchase price. In the coming pages, we'll describe one method that considers **pro forma EBITDA** (as defined in Chapter 10) and another that considers net working capital levels.

> **Expert Insight:**
>
> **Purchase price mechanisms**
>
> Depending on the type of business, the purchase price may be tied to EBITDA, net working capital, a combination thereof, or another metric that's relevant to your business. The mechanism used to determine the final purchase price will be negotiated with your buyer. Be aware of the pros and cons of each and how they relate to your business and might impact the amount of proceeds you receive at closing.

Valuation is the first step in determining a purchase price. Valuation under the income approach is based on expected future cash flows. In order to determine whether those future cash flows are reasonable and achievable, the buyer will first look at your historical cash flows (generally EBITDA) and make adjustments to arrive at pro forma EBITDA.

Using that pro forma EBITDA as a starting point (or baseline), cash flows are projected and used to calculate a value for your business. That value will be compared to your **normalized EBITDA** to determine a "multiple" of normalized EBITDA.

For example, let's assume the buyer performs diligence on your TTM September 30th EBITDA numbers and the closing date of the sale is on November 30th. Using TTM September 30th data, the buyer's valuation of your business is $4 million and your normalized EBITDA is $1 million. That would imply that the buyer is willing to pay four times ("4x") your normalized TTM EBITDA.

Once the buyer establishes the valuation and the multiple, there are a variety of ways he or she could negotiate your purchase price. We show you two examples below.

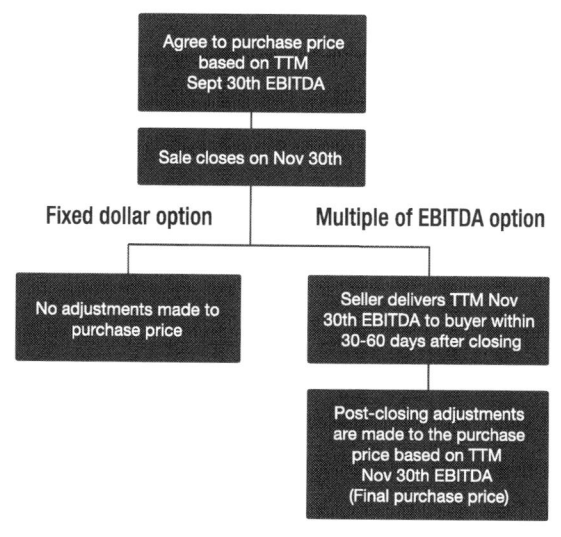

```
┌─────────────────────────────┐
│  Agree to purchase price    │
│      based on TTM           │
│    Sept 30th EBITDA         │
└─────────────┬───────────────┘
              │
┌─────────────▼───────────────┐
│  Sale closes on Nov 30th    │
└──┬───────────────────────┬──┘
   │                       │
Fixed dollar option    Multiple of EBITDA option
   │                       │
┌──▼──────────────┐   ┌────▼────────────────────┐
│ No adjustments  │   │ Seller delivers TTM Nov │
│  made to        │   │ 30th EBITDA to buyer    │
│  purchase price │   │ within 30-60 days after │
│                 │   │ closing                 │
└─────────────────┘   └────────────┬────────────┘
                                   │
                      ┌────────────▼────────────┐
                      │ Post-closing adjustments│
                      │ are made to the purchase│
                      │ price based on TTM      │
                      │ Nov 30th EBITDA         │
                      │ (Final purchase price)  │
                      └─────────────────────────┘
```

1. <u>Fixed dollar option</u> – Using the example above, the buyer would agree to pay you $4 million at closing based on normalized TTM EBITDA as of September 30th. There would be no adjustments to the price for any changes in the TTM EBITDA between September 30th through the closing date on November 30th. In this case, the multiple of 4x is simply a data point used by the buyer to determine whether it's a reasonable price. It is not used to calculate the purchase price.
2. <u>Multiple of EBITDA option</u> – Using the example above, the buyer would agree to pay you 4x normalized EBITDA as of the closing date, November 30th. This means that if your normalized EBITDA as of November 30th is $1.2 million, you'd be paid $4.8 million (4 x $1.2 million) versus the $4 million. Conversely, if your normalized EBITDA at closing is $800,000, the final purchase price would be $3.2 million.

In the multiple of EBITDA option, there could be post-closing adjustments to the initial $4 million purchase price. These adjustments relate to changes in normalized EBITDA between September 30th and November 30th.

- At closing, a portion of the $4 million would likely be put into escrow by the buyer (e.g., 10% or $400,000) to account for any post-closing adjustments to the purchase price.
- The seller has a period of time after closing (generally 30-60 days) to provide the final normalized EBITDA as of November 30th to the buyer.
- The buyer then has 30-60 days to review and agree to the final number.
- Once the final amount is agreed upon, the buyer either (i) pays the additional purchase price, or (ii) the shortfall is taken out of the escrow, reducing the proceeds to the seller.

> **Expert Insight:**
> **Prepare for post-closing adjustments to the purchase price**
>
> How your final purchase price is calculated and the nature of any post-closing adjustments will be negotiated with the buyer during the process. As a seller, you should consider what you expect your results to be between signing and closing. This could potentially impact how you want to structure the purchase price calculation and the final proceeds you receive.

Net working capital requirements

In addition to or instead of post-closing adjustments related to a multiple of EBITDA, there can also be adjustments for net working capital or net asset value. Net working capital (broadly defined as current assets minus current liabilities) is the liquidity that is used to support day-to-day operations of your business.

A buyer might require a minimum level of net working capital in the business at closing to ensure there are no liquidity issues right after closing for the new owner. This is separate from the calculation of the overall purchase price based on normalized EBITDA and is negotiated as a separate component of the purchase price.

Continuing the example above, assume that at September 30th, you had $2 million of current assets and $1.5 million of current liabilities. Your net working capital would be $500,000. There are a couple of options you might negotiate:

1. <u>Minimum net working capital requirement</u> – Under this scenario, you would agree to have at least $500,000 in net working capital on your balance sheet as of November 30th, the closing date. If you had only $450,000 at closing, you would need to pay an additional $50,000 to the buyer for this shortfall. This amount would generally be taken out of the escrow if there were sufficient funds in escrow. If you have more than $500,000 in net working capital, there is no adjustment (i.e., you don't get paid for delivering more net working capital than you agreed to deliver).
2. <u>Dollar-for-dollar net working capital adjustment</u> – In a dollar-for-dollar net working capital adjustment, you would pay the buyer for any shortfall below the $500,000 required net working capital and the buyer would pay you any excess over the $500,000.

Although it seems obvious that, as a seller, you would prefer the dollar-for-dollar adjustment, the more common approach we see is the minimum requirement option. Either way, make sure you know the pros and cons of each approach and have a good understanding of what you expect your net working capital to be at closing before agreeing to any thresholds.

> **Expert Insight:**
>
> **How to define net working capital**
>
> Although the definition of net working capital seems straight forward (current assets minus current liabilities), in reality, the definition of what is included in net working capital is often a major negotiating point with the buyer. The buyer may not want to pay for liabilities that relate to the prior performance of the business (e.g., accrued bonuses for the prior year or accrued vacation) and will want them excluded from the definition of net working capital. Alternatively, the buyer may leave them in the definition but want a reduction in the final purchase price for those amounts. Regardless, make sure you work with your advisors and the buyer to clearly define what is included in net working capital if that is part of your purchase price calculation.

What we've discussed is only a sample of ways to calculate your purchase price. Use your advisors to help determine the best method for your particular situation.

Buyer assessment: selecting the best buyer (it's not just about price)

As you and your team are populating the data room and preparing your management presentation for Phase II Diligence, you will begin fielding questions and reviewing initial indications of interest from buyers.

> **Expert Insight:**
>
> **Communicating with advisors and potential buyers**
>
> This is often when panic sets in and you start wondering:
> - Shouldn't more buyers be interested?
> - Should I be considering the offers I am getting?
> - Do the offers meet my needs for the next step?
>
> Communication of status throughout the process is key to keeping you sane and focused on your business. Your advisor should apprise you of conversations they have with potential buyers, any issues or concerns buyers are expressing, and whether the offers or level of interest are above or below their expectations.

At this point, you're anxious to get the process done, and you'll be tempted to move forward quickly with the highest price. Be careful. The highest-priced buyer may not achieve the exit goals you established for yourself personally and financially. You'll need to understand how each option meets those goals. As you think through the various options presented by potential buyers, ask yourself questions, such as:

- Do the price and structure meet the exit goals I've laid out for myself?
- Do I feel comfortable the buyer has the ability to close?
- Do I clearly understand the assumptions the buyer is using to value my company? Am I concerned these assumptions will change during Phase II Diligence?
- Will I continue in some capacity with the company and do I want to?

There are also the "softer" questions you'll ask, such as:

- Do I feel good about selling my life's work to this buyer?
- Is there a cultural fit with our companies?
- If the buyer plans to retain my brand, am I comfortable with how my brand will be represented in the market?
- How will the buyer treat my employees and customers who have become such an important part of my life over the years?

Only you can answer these questions by doing your own diligence on the buyer. If these questions are important to you, take the time to get to know your potential buyer and don't be afraid to ask the questions most important to you.

Once you select a buyer and sign an LOI, you will still ask questions, but your options are limited to either accepting the answers or stopping the process. Make sure you get enough information prior to signing the LOI to be comfortable moving forward with the buyer.

> **Expert Insight:**
>
> ### Get to know your potential buyer
>
> You need to gain as much knowledge as possible about your potential buyer before signing the LOI. Below are a few of the questions you and/or your transaction advisor should ask:
>
> - What are the buyer's strategic and business objectives for my business?
> - Can the buyer get the funding or does the buyer already have the funding to buy my company?
> - Who has to approve the buyer's purchase of my business? How long will it take to get approval?
> - Does the timing for closing meet my best interests?
> - What is the buyer's history in getting transactions done?
> - Can I talk to business owners who have previously sold their businesses to this buyer?
>
> Phase I Diligence is a two-way street. Ask now, or....

Online Resources: Selecting a buyer

The pendulum swings – control shifts to the buyer

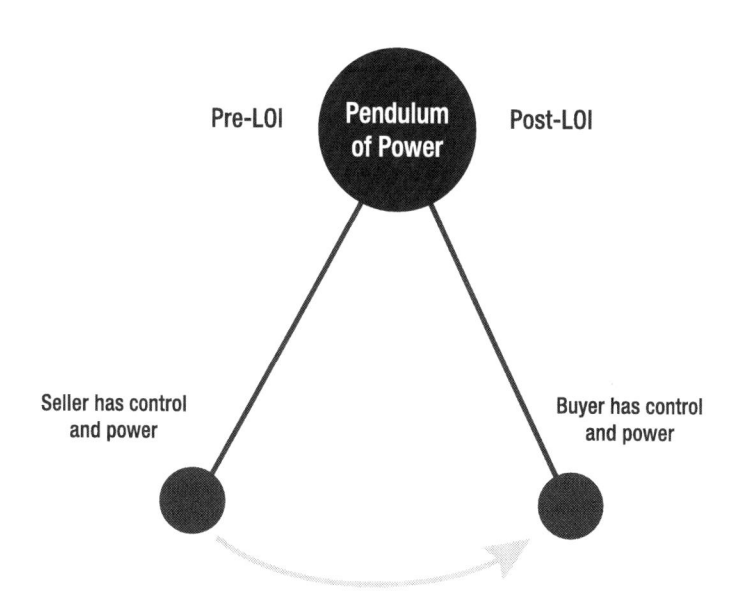

Pendulum of Power

Pre-LOI: Seller has control and power
Post-LOI: Buyer has control and power

Once you select a buyer and sign the LOI, the pendulum of power will swing. You will now be on the defensive side, trying to support the pricing/valuation that was agreed to in the LOI. If you're not well prepared, the pendulum will swing wide and you'll feel a loss of control over the process. This is where re-trade risk is at its highest.

Remember, the buyer's goal is to negotiate the best price from a purchaser's perspective, not necessarily what you think is the "fair" price. There's nothing wrong with that. This is simply a business transaction for the buyer. Make sure you're ready for Phase II Diligence prior to signing the LOI. As soon as you sign the LOI, the game changes and the buyer will want to move quickly into the next phase.

Gut Check: Are you ready to sign the LOI?

Before signing the LOI, make sure you've accomplished the following:
- Understand and be able to support the buyer's detailed assumptions behind the LOI price.
- Practice your management presentation until you can't get it wrong.
- Finish populating the data room and review all documents for accuracy and consistency.
- Be prepared with your communication plan to address questions internally and externally going forward.

If you've completed the above steps, then you're ready to move to the most critical stage of the sale process – Phase II Diligence.

23

Phase II Diligence – buckle your seatbelt!

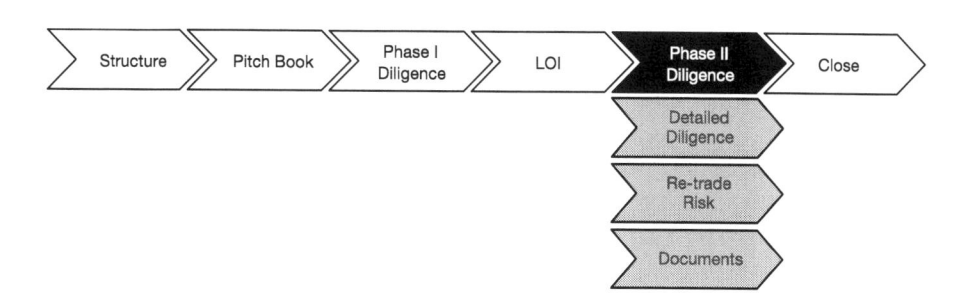

Structure › Pitch Book › Phase I Diligence › LOI › **Phase II Diligence** › Close

Detailed Diligence
Re-trade Risk
Documents

Congratulations! You've found a buyer and entered into an LOI. You're ready to close the deal and get on with your life. High fives all around!

You may feel like you're on the final stretch, but the buyer has just come off the starting blocks.

By gathering data and anticipating buyer questions, you've analyzed your company in so many different ways you probably know more about it now than you ever did. Now, imagine if you had only 30 to 60 days to learn everything you needed to know to run your business successfully and you were starting from ground zero. This is your buyer's challenge. Your goal is to help the buyer learn your business while defending the price agreed to in the LOI.

> **Gut Check: Preparing for the "unexpected" questions**
>
> Are you prepared to begin answering questions from your employees, customers, suppliers and even your neighbors? Get out your communication plan, which you developed while preparing your business (see Part II), and review the potential questions and practice your responses to each possible inquiry. You've already involved your senior management team and hired advisors, so word could get out that you're selling your business. Your employees are going to be concerned for their jobs. Your customers and suppliers are going to wonder whether they'll continue to do business with a new owner. As for your neighbors, that's how rumors get started. Be prepared!

All your hard work has been worth it

All of the hard work you've done since engaging your advisors (preparing the pitch book, compiling the data room, and practicing your management presentations) will finally pay off. Typically, you'll kick off Phase II Diligence by giving your management presentation to the buyer and the buyer's advisors (if you haven't already done so earlier in the process). All the detailed information you put into the data room will be available to the buyer, and the buyer will begin Phase II Diligence on your company and your management team.

Below are the typical activities during Phase II Diligence:

- Seller makes management presentations to the buyer and the buyer's team of advisors, if applicable
- Initial face-to-face meetings are arranged between the buyer and your management team based on function (accounting, operations, sales, etc.)

- Buyer submits/asks questions on the information in the data room
- Buyer asks for additional data and submits follow-up questions regarding the new data (this happens continuously throughout the process)
- Buyer's attorney performs legal review of your documents
- Buyer and seller negotiate potential pricing adjustments
- Buyer and seller finalize the structure of the transaction
- Attorneys draft the purchase documents and other relevant agreements (employment, non-compete, etc.)

These activities seem fairly straightforward, and would be if they happened consecutively instead of simultaneously. Don't forget, you've still got a business to run and now you *and* your management team have taken on a second full-time job of selling the business. Remaining in control of the sale process and your emotions are critical to your success in closing the sale. You can do it, because you're prepared.

Maintain control over the process

A key factor in maintaining control over the process is appointing a single contact person (either your advisor or someone from your team) who is responsible for minimizing disruption of your team's regular job responsibilities. The role of the contact person is to:

- Create and enforce an agenda for the process.
- Coordinate questions and requests for additional data from the buyer.
- Set up meetings or phone calls for the buyer to discuss questions with the relevant members of your team.

As we discussed earlier, one of the benefits of a virtual data room is that the buyer's team doesn't have on-site access that can be disruptive to your team. Instead:

- The buyer reviews the materials offsite and submits lists of questions and data requests through the contact person.
- The buyer and their advisors don't unexpectedly walk into your team's offices with questions throughout the day.
- You can track what documents your buyer is reviewing, which may give you a sense of their concerns and allow you to be proactive in addressing them.

If you decide on a physical data room, you can still require the buyer to submit questions and schedule meetings. It's simply more difficult to control the process if the buyer's team is down the hall from your team.

To stay focused on your business and make the best use of everyone's time, both your team's and the buyer's, create an agenda and stick to it (as closely as possible). The agenda, managed by your primary contact person, should outline when and how the buyer accesses your team to minimize disruption to the business while still cooperating with the buyer. This is a fine line to walk with the buyer, and it doesn't hurt to point out to the buyer that your continued focus on the business is to everyone's advantage.

You want to help the buyer get the relevant information, but your business still needs to be managed. To maintain as much order as possible:

- Create a calendar for meetings that specifies who on your team and the buyer's team will meet, as well as the time and subject of the meeting.
- Ask the buyer to submit questions in advance, so your team has time to gather and review the information prior to the meeting.
- Stick to the schedule. If you don't finish within the specified time, schedule a follow-up meeting another time.

Staying on schedule will help your team manage the time spent on diligence versus running the business. It's difficult to stick to a strict schedule in such a fluid and intense process. Not allowing meetings to go too long or too late into the night will give your team a sense of certainty of their schedule and help keep them motivated.

> **Online Resources: Example diligence calendar**

How do I keep my team motivated?

Keeping your team motivated during this exhausting process is critical. Agendas and schedules are helpful, but how do you keep employees motivated if they're not sure whether they will be offered a job with the new owner?

There are several options/decisions your management team will face during the sale process:

- Accept a job offer from the new owner in the same position
- Accept a job offer from the new owner in a different position
- Be offered a job but choose to leave upon the sale
- Stay through a defined transition period after the sale
- Leave before the sale is completed

Although you may have little or no control over any of your employees' options, try to avoid losing key management while you're trying to sell your business. Losing employees could significantly change the value of the deal to the buyer.

What can happen when key employees leave ...

We worked on a transaction where the seller's top sales person, Susan, left early in the diligence phase. The buyer had planned to retain Susan to solidify critical customer relationships. The buyer became concerned about the strength of customer relationships after the anticipated change of ownership and questioned whether the projected revenue was attainable. After failing to negotiate a re-trade of the price with the seller due to uncertainty surrounding the loss of Susan, the buyer decided not to move forward with the transaction.

There was a similar example related to David, an IT engineer who was instrumental in product development. During diligence, David was offered a job from another company and hadn't been told whether he would be offered a job with the new owner of his current company. He didn't want to risk not having a job and accepted the offer with the other company. The buyer viewed David as potentially key to the future of the company but was not far enough along in diligence to offer him a position. The buyer had to determine whether David's knowledge could be replaced and at what cost. The additional cost and estimated time involved with replacing David and training a new employee resulted in a reduction in the purchase price.

> **Expert Insight:**
>
> **Protect the "value" of your team**
> Buyers are often purchasing your team as much as your business. Communicate early and often with the buyer regarding potential employment for your team. If any of your employees are at risk of leaving prior to completing the sale, let the buyer know. If the buyer is anticipating offering your team positions, encourage the buyer to talk to your team as early as possible.

Stay bonuses

One way to minimize the risk of losing key employees is to establish "stay" or "retention" bonuses. Stay bonuses provide an incentive for employees to stay with the company for a specified period of time (either up to closing or for a transition period after closing) to assist with diligence and, potentially, integration after the sale. Stay bonuses can be a set dollar amount or a percentage of the employee's base salary and are generally paid out at the end of the specified period. If you're planning to provide stay bonuses, discuss this with the buyer to make sure you're spending your dollars wisely on the employees most valuable to you and the buyer.

As we've pointed out, diligence is a time-consuming process for your team. Although it goes against every business owner's philosophy to incur the cost of hiring more people, you may need to hire some part-time help during this process. It's a cost to you, but it allows your business to continue to grow, your team to stay motivated, and, possibly, speeds up the diligence process.

> **Expert Insight:**
> ### Time kills deals
> When you sell a house, the longer it's on the market, the lower the likelihood it will sell for the price you want. The same goes for businesses. The longer diligence drags on, the higher the risk of re-trade and the less likely you and the buyer will come to agreement on price and terms. It's a delicate balance between getting the deal done quickly, keeping your team motivated, and keeping your foot on the accelerator of your business.

Surviving diligence – being prepared for re-trade risk

> **Expert Insight:**
>
> **Phase II Diligence is the most difficult phase for the seller**
>
> You've put your life into this company and you're proud of what you and your team have accomplished. The buyer will not necessarily see or appreciate the blood, sweat and tears that have built your business over time. The difference in your view of the value of your business and the buyer's can create anxiety for you and a lot of tension between the two of you.

This is where re-trade risk becomes a reality. Items found during Phase II Diligence can mean adjustments to the purchase price that you agreed to in the LOI.

This is the most personal thing you'll ever do in business, and it's critical you don't take it personally!

Phase II Diligence is where the process gets very personal for sellers. Somebody will likely call your "baby" ugly. The buyer is questioning everything you do and wants support for your answers. Your word is not enough.

Although we can't tell you exactly what a potential buyer will ask you and your team, we know the following to be true:

- Diligence is always more time-consuming than you anticipate.
- It will feel like the buyer wants more detail than needed and more than you want to give.

- You'll question why the buyer wants certain information.
- You'll get defensive about the buyer's questions on decisions you've made or processes you've put in place.
- You and your team will become frustrated and worn out by the constant questions while still trying to run the business.

> **Expert Insight:**
>
> **How to avoid getting defensive**
>
> Remember that you know and understand your business intuitively; the buyer does not. Of course, the buyer's goal is to buy the business for the best price possible. Listening to and understanding the buyer's valuation assumptions and assessment of certain risks or liabilities might allow you both an opportunity for clarification and reassessment. We find the best way to respond to difficult questions is to say something like: "Help me understand what you're looking for so I can help answer your questions." This simple sentence puts you and the buyer on the same team and working toward the same goal of understanding the underlying issue. It also provides you a chance to breathe before you react defensively to a buyer's question.

You'll survive intact because you're prepared

Most sellers don't realize the tension they're about to endure, or that the issues above kill deals more often than pricing differences. Sometimes, diligence simply becomes too much for the seller's management team and the process breaks down. You're probably asking yourself: "How will I manage these issues and keep running my business successfully?" This is where preparation pays off. You can manage expectations and avoid some of the common emotional pitfalls of diligence because you have taken the critical and necessary time to prepare yourself and prepare your business.

Here are a few tips to deal with the emotional roller coaster that occurs during diligence:

- Don't take it personally (easier said than done). Your buyer isn't questioning your integrity (hopefully), but trying to understand as much about your company as possible in a short period of time.
- Be prepared *prior* to beginning Phase II Diligence. Know your data and information down to a very detailed level.
- Look at your data objectively and anticipate questions before they are asked. What are the next three levels of details the buyer will need? Can you provide and support that information?
- Never let your guard down. Everything you say during the sale process could impact the transaction. Be factual and keep everything on a business level.
- Ask the buyer a lot of questions. Get to know the plans the buyer has for your company and how your management team may fit in. Remain engaged in the overall process.

Diligence can be very detailed and require a lot of patience on your part and the part of your team as you answer the buyer's questions. Here's an example of the types of questions you might be asked on just one item on your balance sheet, accounts receivable:

You receive an initial data request from the buyer and provide a list of outstanding receivables from your customers, including the date of invoices. The buyer may have these initial follow up questions to your list:

- *What are your standard collection terms for receivables? (30 days)*
- *Explain the reason why some of the receivables on the list are past 30 days.*

- *Who's responsible for collecting receivables? How successful is that effort?*
- *Do you charge interest on overdue receivables?*
- *Have you ever written off a receivable (i.e., forgiven the amount due)? If yes, please provide a list of those customers and the reason for the write-off. Are you still doing business with those customers? Why?*
- *Please provide a list of your largest customers for the past three years. Explain why you lost some customers during that time frame. Is it a product/service quality issue? Are you losing market share to your competitors?*
- *Why are some of your largest customers overdue on their invoices? Do you provide them with different terms than other customers?*
- *Do you have written contracts with all of your customers or are some arrangements verbal? Which customers have verbal arrangements?*

How would you feel if you couldn't answer some of these questions, or if the buyer asked this many questions on ten items on your balance sheet? Twenty items? If you let your emotions take over, the conversation will likely not be productive with the buyer.

> **Expert Insight:**
>
> ## Prepare for the "big picture" questions
>
> We've been focusing on making sure you're prepared for the detailed questions about your business, but you must also be prepared to answer strategic questions such as:
> - If you had additional capital, what would be your first priority for growing the business?
> - What are the top three opportunities and challenges you see for your business in the short term and long term?
> - What type of budgeting and planning processes do you have in place?
> - If you could change one aspect of the business, what would it be? What has stopped you from making that change already?
>
> These are the types of questions you must be prepared to answer in addition to the more detailed and tactical questions that would come from the IRL. Whether you have the information formally documented or it's in your head, show the buyer you know your business issues and help shape the buyer's view of the value of the business.

The buyer wants to negotiate purchase adjustments

This is where re-trade risk will become a reality. You feel like you've answered every question the buyer has asked; you've made your team available; and you've been incredibly helpful to the buyer in the process. After all that, you're now going to have to defend the purchase price you agreed to in the LOI? You now have to take three very important steps: take a deep breath, listen intently, and ask clarifying questions. Remember, this isn't personal.

Is there a communication void or error, miscommunication, or need for deeper understanding or clarification of the issue? Ask questions to more deeply understand the buyer's perspective and how the risk was quantified. Then share with the buyer your experience and explain how you've mitigated that risk in the past. The goal here is to influence the buyer's perception of the risk and minimize the discount related to that risk.

> **Expert Insight:**
>
> ### Understand your buyer's projection assumptions
>
> Many sellers never ask or gain an understanding of the assumptions used by the buyer in their valuation model. Arm yourself with information regarding the buyer's projections for your business, so you can proactively address matters that might result in a re-trade of the LOI price. Consider running their assumptions through your own valuation tool to see what the impact might be on the final price. Be prepared with arguments to support the price you want.

For example, a buyer may determine your reliance on a large customer for 40% of your sales is a key risk. The buyer will be asking: "What if the customer decides to move its business to a competitor after the change in ownership? Will I be able to replace those sales with new customers? How long will that take?" If you're not prepared for these questions and you're at a high point on the emotional roller coaster, it would be easy to overreact and not be able to ease the buyer's concerns.

If you've taken the time to prepare your business, you've likely identified customer concentration as a potential risk and are prepared to answer this concern. Maybe your largest customer is in a long-term contract with you that is difficult to terminate. If you're far enough along in the process, you might feel comfortable allowing the buyer to talk to your customer about continuing business after the sale. Bottom line, don't panic or get defensive. Be prepared for these types of questions and flatten your emotional roller coaster.

What other types of issues can result in a purchase price adjustment?

The buyer may discover:

- A potential liability isn't recorded on your books (e.g., legal claim from one of your employees that is still outstanding).
- Your equipment is old and outdated and will need to be replaced.
- There are several accounts receivable that are older than one year and need to be written off.
- The lease payments on your facility increase significantly within the next 12 months.

This is just a sample of items that might arise and could negatively impact your purchase price. Hopefully, you identified these issues while you were preparing your business through the *eyes of the buyer* and factored the potential reductions into your expected price before you entered into the LOI. If not, you may be facing the choice of accepting a lower price or ending negotiations with this buyer and starting the process over again.

> **Expert Insight:**
>
> ### Your deal will "die" at least once
>
> During diligence and discussions around purchase price adjustments, it's not uncommon for a deal to die two or three times. You and the buyer may disagree on the nature or amount of a potential price adjustment, and it may feel as if the differences are too great to overcome. This is when the emotional roller coaster is in high gear. Your best defense is a good offense. Simply by knowing this will probably happen at some point in the process, you will be much better prepared for it.
> - Know ahead of time what you're willing to negotiate.
> - Be open to alternatives presented by the buyer.
> - Discuss the alternatives with your advisors.
> - Understand how your exit goals will be impacted by potential changes in terms or purchase price.
>
> Knowing what to expect is half the battle.

What documents will I need to sign?

During Phase II Diligence, you'll need to start drafting the documents for the closing. When we say "you," we really mean you and your advisors. Generally, your attorney is responsible for drafting the documents and should have a fairly standard template to get started. If you're dealing with an experienced buyer, the buyer's attorney may draft it instead. While other documents may be needed, the typical documents in a sale process include:

- Purchase and Sale Agreement – primary sale document
- Non-compete agreement, if applicable
- Employment agreement/consulting agreement, if applicable

Purchase and sale agreement

The primary document for the transaction will be the Purchase and Sale Agreement ("PSA"). This document can also be referred to as the "Definitive Agreement." The PSA finalizes the terms of the transaction that were initially outlined in the LOI and is typically laid out in the following order:

- *Deal provisions* – terms and structure of the transaction, including price and form of payment.
- *Representations and warranties* – details what is being sold and in what condition. Buyer and seller represent they have the ability to move forward with the transaction (i.e., buyer will have financing and seller has clean title to the assets being sold). Generally, the representations and warranties survive the closing. If you breach them, you are in breach of the entire contract.
- *Covenants* – actions for the seller and buyer to take (or not take) between signing and closing. Generally, this requires the seller to run the business "as normal."
- *Conditions to closing* – conditions that have to be met by the seller and buyer before closing. Often this requires the buyer to obtain financing.
- *Termination provision* – conditions upon which the transaction can be terminated and the break-up fees are to be paid upon termination.
- *Disclosure schedules* – detailed schedules attached as appendices to the PSA that typically discuss exceptions to the PSA. For example, the PSA might state: "The buyer will acquire all the assets and liabilities of the company except for those assets and liabilities listed on Schedule 1.3." Your Schedule 1.3 would list the assets and liabilities that will not be sold to the buyer.

Representations (reps) and warranties

The list of reps and warranties can be extensive and would seem to be straightforward. Don't overlook it. This is still a contract and you will be legally responsible for answering truthfully. Most of the reps will have a related disclosure schedule in the appendix. Review those in detail and make sure they're accurate.

If any of the reps and warranties turns out to be false, you may owe money to the buyer (an indemnity). The basis for claims under the indemnity will be set up in the contract. Understand how much liability you are taking on for the reps and warranties.

The buyer will generally require a percentage of the purchase consideration be set aside in escrow to back up the indemnities, usually for one year. The percentage is often 10% of the total purchase price, but can be more or less depending on what is negotiated. The escrow is the money the buyer can claim based on the indemnities without having to actually sue the seller. The escrow can also be used for post-closing adjustments to the purchase price discussed earlier.

Drafting the PSA

Your attorney and other advisors should be involved in drafting the PSA. Depending on the complexity of your business and the terms of your deal, the PSA can become quite long and detailed. As a seller, you should first focus on the following high-level questions:

- Do the price and terms in the PSA make sense to you, and are they aligned with your exit objectives?
- Are you able to make all of the representations and warranties that are in the document?
- Do you anticipate any material changes in your business that would make you break any of the covenants in the PSA? The requirement to continue running your business as normal could include limitations on the size of contracts you can sign or limitations on capital expenditures.
- Can you meet all of your conditions to closing? Are you comfortable the buyer can get the financing to close on the sale?
- Have you fully disclosed all information required in the disclosure schedules, including any exceptions to the representations and warranties?

Other agreements

Depending on the structure of your transaction and whether you plan to have a role with the company going forward, there are other agreements you may enter into. These agreements will be specific to each case and, like the PSA, should be drafted by your legal advisor. The following are just some of the agreements you might enter into at closing.

Non-compete agreement – If you will be exiting the company, the buyer may want to make sure you don't take your client relationships down the street and set up shop as a competitor. A non-compete agreement pays you not to work in the same industry and/or geography for a specified period of time (generally one to five years). Before you sign the non-compete, make sure the limitations are specific and the time frame is reasonable. Note that several states discourage the use of non-compete agreements, including California, which will not enforce them. Ask your legal advisor what rules apply in your state. A non-compete clause is also often included in employment agreements.

Employment agreement – Employment agreements allow the seller to become an employee of the new company and continue with certain benefits such as health insurance, an expense account, company car, etc. This is generally viewed as a short-term solution to assist the new owner's transition and provide the seller a "landing pad" into their new lifestyle. It also requires you to be an *employee* of the new owner with no control over the decision-making process. This can be very frustrating to sellers. Given this risk, sellers more often enter into consulting agreements with the new owner. If you decide on an employment agreement, make sure it's separate from the purchase and sale agreement. If the employment relationship doesn't work out, you want the overall transaction to survive.

There are several items to negotiate in an employment agreement, including:

- Term of the agreement (how long you will be employed)
- Compensation (salary and benefits)
- Responsibilities and duties. These will be different from your previous responsibilities as the owner. Make sure they are detailed and clear to all parties.
- Termination (severance or other termination benefits)

Consulting agreement - Consulting agreements are most common when selling your company to a third party (versus management). They allow you to earn additional income over the period of the agreement (generally one to two years) and allow the buyer to deduct the payments as compensation expense for tax purposes. The arrangement generally requires the seller to be on call for any questions or issues the new owner might have, but is not a full-time commitment. You still get paid even if you are never asked for your time.

Another use of a consulting agreement could be to bridge the gap in pricing between you and the buyer by paying additional proceeds to the seller via a consulting agreement over a period of time.

> **Gut Check: Am I ready to close?**
> Am I ready to sign the documents and move to closing? Do I feel good about my post-closing plan? Are my communication plans in place? Before you sign any documents, make sure you've asked and answered these questions.

24

Closing – you beat the Exit Bubble™!

Structure → Pitch Book → Phase I Diligence → LOI → Phase II Diligence → **Close**

The big moment has arrived!

The negotiations may have gone long into the night, and you've finally agreed to the final points in the transaction documents. Your communication plan and FAQs are ready to go and you've coordinated with the buyer on how to announce the transaction. You've given your wiring instructions to the buyer and you are ready to close the deal!

You've probably been dreaming of the moment when you would sit next to the buyer, sign multiple documents, exchange handshakes and be euphoric over actually completing the process of selling your company. That may not be how it actually plays out.

It's possible (and likely) that you will not even see the buyer at closing. Instead, you may sign the documents at your office or your attorney's office and fax your signatures to the buyer. The buyer would do the same. You might even have pre-signed some of the documents the night before, and the most exciting part of the day will be an e-mail from your bank confirming the wire or check from the buyer has cleared.

This new, more efficient closing process may leave you feeling a bit let down after all the negotiations and stress you've been through over the past several months. The letdown could turn to fear and dread if you haven't already determined a clear plan for yourself after closing. If you've not prepared yourself sufficiently as covered in *Part I*, this could be a very sad day and the beginning of a tough stretch in your life.

> **Gut Check: Can you answer "now what"?**
>
> After the closing, can you answer "now what?" with a sense of excitement, or is it with a sense of fear and uncertainty? Have you created a clear vision of who you are and what you will be after you exit your business? If not, this could be one of the worst days of your life and it could make actually signing on the dotted line difficult for you. It's why we stress the importance of preparing yourself financially and emotionally for your exit (see Part I).

Day 1 of the rest of your life

It's time to execute on the "now what" – what does that mean to you? If you sell and immediately exit, your "what's next" will be different than if you sell but stay on as an employee or consultant for a while. There might also be a longer transition period if you've decided to transition your business to the next generation or create an ESOP for your employees to purchase your business over time.

Regardless of your strategy, you should already have a plan in place for the "big stuff" related to your exit: your financial plan and your longer-term personal goals. Try not to sweat the small stuff. Your biggest decision on the day after you exit is hopefully what to eat for breakfast.

We recommend you have a general plan in place for the first 100 days after you exit. This could include something as simple as taking a short trip with your family or reconnecting with friends. Maybe you want to do some low-key house projects. Just don't find yourself getting up that morning and having no plan for the day. You don't want to start having "seller's remorse" and questioning what you've done and why you've done it!

> **Expert Insight:**
>
> **You don't have to invest your proceeds immediately**
>
> If you received a lump sum payment, don't worry about investing it all the minute the wire clears. Financial advisors often recommend leaving it cash or something liquid for a period of time after closing. Ninety days will not make or break your retirement fund and will give you time to make informed choices. Take your time and enjoy your success!

If you've taken the right steps and have prepared yourself for what's next, this day should be a great beginning for you and your family. By preparing yourself and preparing your business, you successfully exited your business. You are the one of the one-in-four business owners who beat the Exit Bubble™. Now it's time to smile, relax and enjoy – you've earned it!

Key takeaways from Part III – Exit your business:
- Focus on what you *can* control in the process.
- Understand the difference between an asset sale and stock sale on your taxes and exit objectives.
- Earn-outs can bridge the gap in pricing but there is a risk you might never receive those payments.
- A pitch book should tell the story of your business with enough detail to make buyers want to learn more.
- To maintain negotiating power, identify negative issues in your business early while you still have multiple bidders.
- Don't underestimate the importance of management presentations – practice until you can't get it wrong.
- The best buyer is not necessarily the highest bidder.
- When you sign the letter of intent, the power of negotiation generally swings to the buyer.
- You can't take diligence personally.
- Don't sign any documents without help from your advisors.
- Know what's next for you so you don't suffer a letdown after closing.

Online resources referenced in Part III:
Buying this book gives you **free access** to online resources available through your Book Level Membership of **ExitBubble.com**, including, but not limited to, the resources referenced in *Part III*:
- Tips for negotiating earn-outs
- Top 10 tips for pitch books
- Sample information request list
- Comparison of virtual and physical data rooms

- Tips for protecting sensitive information
- Selecting a buyer
- Example diligence calendar

Go deeper in Exit Bubble Elite

Exit Bubble Elite provides you additional in-depth and personalized resources such as:

- Pitch book template that walks you through each section of the pitch book.
- Expanded sample information request list that includes explanations of each item as well as potential questions a buyer might ask for each item.
- Scenarios for calculating a purchase price
- Sample transaction documents (LOI, PSA, non-compete, employment, consulting agreements), including tips for negotiating.

Exit Bubble Elite

We could only scratch the surface of the Exit Bubble™ in this book. Our goal was to provide you enough information on the key aspects of exiting your business that you can make more informed decisions when navigating the Exit Bubble™, including knowing when and how to engage the appropriate advisors for you and your business.

Don't forget to use the ***FREE Online Resources*** that are referenced throughout the book. Our online resources provide a tremendous amount of additional information that will help you during this process, including tips from experts and lessons learned from business owners who have been in your shoes.

If you'd like to delve deeper into this subject, we've created Exit Bubble Elite – an online resource that provides you with more tools, information and video interviews of other business owners and advisors sharing their experiences. These resources are provided to better help you prepare for all aspects of the exit process including:

Prepare Yourself:

- Emergenetics profile – customized exclusively for Exit Bubble Elite.
    - A personalized assessment of your natural strengths by Emergenetics International, a company specializing in analyzing, identifying and leveraging the way people think and behave.
    - Includes a one-on-one coaching session with a Certified Emergenetics Associate who can help you identify and understand your natural strengths and begin to answer "who am I, if I'm not the owner of my business?"

- Life Path Workbook - exclusive to Exit Bubble Elite
    - Hands-on exercises that will help you apply what you learned through your Emergenetics profile to your plans for "post-exit" life.
- Personal Vault
    - In-depth tool that warehouses all of your critical information in one place, including all of your passwords, financial information, insurance information, and other information you or family may need in a moment's notice.

Prepare Your Business:

- Unlimited access to a comprehensive online valuation. analysis tool with step-by-step video instructions.
- Interactive Value Profile tool included in the online valuation analysis tool.
- Electronic copy of the book *"Ownership Thinking: How to End Entitlement and Create a Culture of Accountability, Purpose, and Profit"* (accompanied by videos) by best-selling author, Brad Hams, who shows you how to increase your company's productivity, employee retention, and profitability.
- Communication plan template with example questions to prepare to answer during your process.

Exit Your Business:

- Pitch book template that walks you through each section of the pitch book.
- Expanded sample information request list that includes explanations of each item as well as potential questions a buyer might ask for each item.
- Scenarios for calculating a purchase price.
- Sample transaction documents (LOI, PSA, non-compete, employment, consulting agreements), including tips for negotiating.

The above items are just a sample of the tools and resources you'll receive in Exit Bubble Elite. As with all of our content on the website, it is delivered via video and in writing, so you can choose the method of delivery that works best for you. If you're interested in learning more, go to our website at **www.ExitBubble.com**.

We hope to see you at **www.ExitBubble.com** and best of luck in your journey!

Glossary of Terms

The following terms are referenced throughout the book.

Asset approach – valuation method based on the fair value of net assets (assets minus liabilities).

Asset sale – the sale of a portion of a company's assets and liabilities.

Book value – the value that assets and liabilities are recorded on the books or financial records of the business.

Capital expenditures (Cap ex) – purchases of capital assets including property, plant and equipment.

C Corporation (C-Corp) – a separate legal entity from the owners that is taxed once at the corporation level and a second time when it is distributed to the owners. Owners get protection from individual liability.

Cost of capital – the cost of a company's funds (debt or equity) or an investor's required rate of return. Also referred to as discount rate when calculating the present value of future cash flows.

Certified Public Accountant (CPA) – a qualified accountant in the United States who has passed the Uniform Certified Public Accountant Examination and met additional requirements for certification.

Diligence – also referred to as "due diligence." An investigative process by the buyer to confirm all material facts of the sale. Also performed on a lesser scale by the seller on the buyer.

Discount rate – the rate used to calculate the present value of future cash flows. Also referred to as cost of capital.

Downshifting – emphasizes finding an improved balance between leisure and work and focusing life goals on personal fulfillment and relationship building instead of the all-consuming pursuit of economic success.

Earn-out – contractual agreement between the seller and buyer that provides for additional compensation to the seller if future "targets" are met. This is a strategy often used to bridge perceived pricing gaps between sellers and buyers.

EBITDA – common term used in sale processes. This represents earnings before interest expense, taxes, depreciation and amortization. Viewed as a good indication of operating cash flows.

Employee Stock Ownership Plan (ESOP) – provides a company's workforce with an ownership interest in the company.

Fair value – price at which the asset could be bought or sold between two parties. Also referred to as market value.

Financial buyer – typically private equity funds, venture capital funds, buyout funds or private investment funds with a set of investors who finance their transactions.

Free Cash Flow (FCF) – cash available after operating costs and investments, but before servicing debt. Cash flow used to pay the business owner a salary and to pay interest and principal on the business' debt.

Goodwill – the difference between the purchase price of a business and the value of its physical assets.

Income approach – valuation method based on today's value of future cash flows available for use. Also called the Discounted Cash Flow Approach.

Intangible value – the value of an asset that can't be seen or touched.

Information request list (IRL) – a list of information typically requested by the buyer at the start of diligence. The checklist is also typically the starting point for the information in the data room.

Key performance indicator (KPI) – a performance measure used to evaluate the success of a specific activity.

Legacy liabilities – liabilities of a business that occurred prior to its sale.

Lifestyle buyer – buyer looking for a business that will support their lifestyle in terms of workload and compensation.

Limited Liability Corporation (LLC) – a legal corporate structure whereby members acquire membership interests versus acquiring shares in a company. Owners enjoy the limited liability a C-Corp offers combined with the single level of taxation a sole proprietorship or partnership offers.

Letter of intent (LOI) – a typically non-binding agreement between a seller and buyer that outlines the general terms of the buyer's offer subject to diligence.

Last twelve months (LTM) – also referred to as TTM; typically used when describing a period of historical financial statements or EBITDA.

Market approach – valuation method based on "multiples" from market transactions (sales) of similar businesses.

Multi-member LLC – an LLC with more than one member or "owner."

Nondisclosure agreement (NDA) – a document that potential buyers sign agreeing to keep confidential any information provided by the seller. This could also be called a confidentiality agreement.

Net assets – total assets minus total liabilities.

Net working capital – current assets minus current liabilities. Can be used as a mechanism to calculate the final purchase price.

Non-compete agreement – agreement made by the seller not to compete in the same business or geography for an agreed-upon period of time.

Non-recurring income or expense – income or expense that is a "one-time" item and / or is not expected to continue in the future.

Normalized EBITDA – EBITDA adjusted for non-recurring or extraordinary items on a historical basis. Generally used for calculating final purchase price calculations.

Normalizing adjustments - take into account non-recurring or one-time items (either revenue or expense) that occurred in historical financial statements but would not be expected to continue in the future.

Partnership – A business organization in which two or more individuals manage and operate the business. Owners are equally and personally liable for the debts from the business.

Present Value (PV) – also known as "discounted value." Represents a future period's cash flow in terms of today's dollar.

Pro forma adjustments – take into account any changes anticipated in the future (versus unusual items that occurred in the past). These include anticipated changes in the existing business (e.g., increase in health care costs) as well as anticipated changes under a new owner (e.g., closing a facility or employee reductions). Pro forma adjustments will be used to present a "baseline" pro forma income statement as if the transaction had occurred at the beginning of each historical period.

Pro forma EBITDA – EBITDA adjusted for pro forma adjustments.

Purchase and sale agreement (PSA) – primary agreement signed by the seller and buyer outlining the terms of the sale of the business. Also referred to as a Definitive Agreement.

Quality of earnings (QofE) – exercise to identify non-recurring and one-time items in historical financial statements to understand the quality of historical reported earnings.

Re-trade risk – risk that based on items found in diligence the buyer would re-negotiate or "re-trade" the price agreed to in the LOI.

S Corporation (S-Corp) – form of legal entity that is taxed at the individual owner level versus the corporation level as in a C-Corp.

Seller financing – a seller may elect to personally finance a portion of the purchase price, to be paid back (generally with interest) over a determined future period.

Selling, general and administrative (SG&A) – operating expenses.

Single member LLC – an LLC with only one member. For tax purposes, this is generally treated like a sole proprietorship.

Sole proprietorship – entity owned by one person that has not been incorporated under any specific type of legal entity such as LLC, partnership, S-Corp or C-Corp.

Stock sale – the sale of 100% of the shares (or partnership / membership interests) of a business.

Strategic buyer – generally a company that already owns a business in the same industry or geography and is looking to expand.

Transaction advisor – a third party engaged by the seller or buyer to assist in the transaction. Could include an attorney, CPA, financial advisor, investment banker or business broker, among others.

Trailing twelve months (TTM) – also referred to as LTM; typically used when describing a period of historical financial statements or EBITDA.

Terminal value (TV) – sometimes referred to as Horizon Value or Continuing Value. TV is a single value that represents the entire present value associated with FCFs beyond the time horizon of annual FCF projections.

Walk-away price – lowest price to be accepted for the sale of the business before the seller "walks away" from the potential buyer and end the sale process.

Weighted average cost of capital (WACC) – average of the costs of financing a company's assets (either debt or equity), each of which is weighted by its respective use. Can be used to determine the discount rate in the income approach to valuation.

References

Reference 1

Number of baby boomer owned businesses:

- U.S. Census Bureau. (2011). *2007 Survey of Business Owners: 2007. (SB0700CSCBO08)*. Retrieved from http://factfinder2.census.gov/faces/tableservices/jsf/pages/productview.xhtml?fpt=table.
- U.S. Census Bureau. (2013). *Nonemployer Statistics:2011*. Retrieved from http://censtats.census.gov/cgi-bin/nonemployer/nonsect.pl.
- U.S. Census Bureau. (2013). *County Business Patterns:2010*. Retrieved from http://www.census.gov/econ/susb/.

Number of businesses transferring ownership in 5 years

- PricewaterhouseCoopers LLP (2013). *PwC Family Business Survey 2012/2013 US Findings*. Retrieved from http://www.pwc.com/us/en/private-company-services/publications/assets/pwc-family-business-survey-us-report.pdf.

Number of businesses transferring ownership in 10 years

- MassMutual, Kennesaw State University, Family Firm Institute (2007). *American Family Business Survey:2007*. Retrieved from http://www.massmutual.com/mmfg/pdf/afbs.pdf.

Reference 2

75% of owners don't have a plan for exiting

- Christman, Peter. Cited in Taylor, Barbara. "*Are Baby Boomers Ready to Exit their Businesses?*" *New York Times*. 10 February 2011.

Reference 3

Retirement savings of boomers

- Employee Benefit Research Institute, Mathew Greenwald & Associates, Inc. (2013) *2013 Retirement Confidence Survey, RCS Fact Sheet #4*. Retrieved from http://www.ebri.org/pdf/surveys/rcs/2013/Final-FS.RCS-13.FS_3.Saving.FINAL.pdf.

Made in the USA
Lexington, KY
08 February 2014